What to
EXPECT
When Your Child
Leaves For
College

A Complete Guide for Parents Only

By
Mary Spohn

What to Expect When Your Child Leaves For College:
A Complete Guide for Parents Only

Copyright © 2008 Atlantic Publishing Group, Inc.
1405 SW 6th Avenue • Ocala, Florida 34471 • Phone 800-814-1132 • Fax 352-622-1875
Web site: www.atlantic-pub.com • E-mail: sales@atlantic-pub.com
SAN Number: 268-1250

ISBN-13: 978-1-60138-218-4   ISBN-10: 1-60138-218-9

Library of Congress Cataloging-in-Publication Data

Spohn, Mary, 1957-
  What to expect when your child leaves for college : a complete guide for parents only / by Mary Spohn.
     p. cm.
  Includes bibliographical references and index.
  ISBN-13: 978-1-60138-218-4 (alk. paper)
  ISBN-10: 1-60138-218-9 (alk. paper)
  1. College students--Family relationships--United States. 2. College student orientation--United States. 3. Parenting--United States. 4. Parent and child--United States. I. Title.

  LB3607.S64 2008
  378.1'98--dc22
                              2008012700

Printed on Recycled Paper

Printed in the United States

Cover Design: Vickie Taylor • vtaylor@atlantic-pub.com

Dedication

"To my three sons, Ian, Stuart, and Christopher. You have filled my life up with happiness and pride. I have enjoyed watching you grow into the wonderful people you are now becoming. I love you always, Mom."

We recently lost our beloved pet "Bear," who was not only our best and dearest friend but also the "Vice President of Sunshine" here at Atlantic Publishing. He did not receive a salary but worked tirelessly 24 hours a day to please his parents. Bear was a rescue dog that turned around and showered myself, my wife Sherri, his grandparents Jean, Bob and Nancy and every person and animal he met (maybe not rabbits) with friendship and love. He made a lot of people smile every day.

We wanted you to know that a portion of the profits of this book will be donated to The Humane Society of the United States.

–Douglas & Sherri Brown

THE HUMANE SOCIETY
OF THE UNITED STATES©

The human-animal bond is as old as human history. We cherish our animal companions for their unconditional affection and acceptance. We feel a thrill when we glimpse wild creatures in their natural habitat or in our own backyard.

Unfortunately, the human-animal bond has at times been weakened. Humans have exploited some animal species to the point of extinction.

The Humane Society of the United States makes a difference in the lives of animals here at home and worldwide. The HSUS is dedicated to creating a world where our relationship with animals is guided by compassion. We seek a truly humane society in which animals are respected for their intrinsic value, and where the human-animal bond is strong.

Want to help animals? We have plenty of suggestions. Adopt a pet from a local shelter, join The Humane Society and be a part of our work to help companion animals and wildlife. You will be funding our educational, legislative, investigative and outreach projects in the U.S. and across the globe.

Or perhaps you'd like to make a memorial donation in honor of a pet, friend or relative? You can through our Kindred Spirits program. And if you'd like to contribute in a more structured way, our Planned Giving Office has suggestions about estate planning, annuities, and even gifts of stock that avoid capital gains taxes.

Maybe you have land that you would like to preserve as a lasting habitat for wildlife. Our Wildlife Land Trust can help you. Perhaps the land you want to share is a backyard—that's enough. Our Urban Wildlife Sanctuary Program will show you how to create a habitat for your wild neighbors.

So you see, it's easy to help animals. And The HSUS is here to help.

The Humane Society of the United States
2100 L Street NW
Washington, DC 20037
202-452-1100
www.hsus.org

Contents

Preface

If you are like most parents with a child embarking on a college career, you have dedicated an enormous amount of your spare time recently to helping your child find and apply to the right college. If your student was applying to more than one college, chances are you had so many deadlines to keep up with — academic applications, scholarships, and financial aid — that you kept a special calendar just to keep up with it all.

You probably began the process of helping your son or daughter explore options during his or her junior year. During senior year, students can become overwhelmed with college deadlines, SATs, final exams, and college campus visits. It can be a challenge to sort out what you need to do, when, and for which college; what entrance exams need to be taken; whether your child needs to audition, try out, or visit in person; and whether your student's grade point average puts him or her in the running for consideration. If you are like most parents, you were probably doing a lot behind the scenes to ease the burden for your high school senior, and you have most likely dedicated all your recent vacation time to visiting schools and attending freshman orientation.

Now that the planning, the strategizing, and the dreaming are finally coming to an end, and your son or daughter is about to leave home for the first time, the reality of it all is beginning to dawn on you. You begin to worry whether you have done enough to prepare your son or daughter for the big, wide world. What if they need medical help? What if they have trouble managing their money? What if they fail calculus? How will they manage? Did you buy them enough towels? Enough T-shirts? And so on.

In fact, you have been so busy worrying how your student will get along, you have not even stopped to consider that your own life is about to be forever changed. For the last year, your entire life has been consumed in helping this child get off on the right foot, and now, overnight, your spare time will go from non-existent, to over-abundant.

So what about you? How will you feel? What will it be like? In this book, we provide some answers and some practical suggestions for overcoming feelings of loneliness and emptiness. We give you insights into what your students are going through, how to support them, how to build up your own life, and how to keep the lines of communication open as the family dynamic transitions from parenting a child to becoming the parent of an adult.

Introduction

I have two sons in college. Ian is 20 and a sophomore at the University of Nebraska (UNL); he is a Biology major, and he plans to go to medical school. Stuart is 18 and a freshman at Georgia Institute of Technology (Georgia Tech) in Atlanta; he is a Mechanical Engineering major, and he will minor in Music. Ian is a National Merit Scholar with a full academic scholarship to UNL and Stu is on the co-op option at Georgia Tech where he will interleave work and study semesters to broaden and help fund his education.

From Ian's junior year at high school until Stu's senior year at high school, all my spare time was dedicated to helping them understand the college application process. How should they choose a college? What should they major in? What is the application process? When do they write the essays? How many times should they take the SAT? Can we use the Common Application? Did the teachers send in the teacher references? In three years, I helped them apply for 10 colleges and get seven acceptance offers — five of those with scholarship offers. I used a dedicated calendar to help them stay on track and spent a lot of time on college Web sites doing research while they focused on getting their homework done, writing the essays, studying for the SATs, and performing their community service.

When they were finally both in college, I sat down and breathed a heavy sigh. I was not used to free time. I missed the boys, and even with one son still at home, I felt the void keenly. If you do not fill your time up, you start to obsess over what they are doing, whether they are happy, and whether they are getting good grades rather than letting them go through the process, learn their own lessons, and carve their own path in life.

SECTION

1

Planning
for the Big
Departure

CHAPTER 1

Leaving High School

As students go through their senior year in high school, many of them are taught to look forward with anticipation to a life of freedom in college where they will choose their own classes, live on their own timetables, have money in their pockets, and get their parents and annoying siblings off their backs. Maybe it ends up that way, and most students grow to love their college experience, but it often does not start out that way.

For some students, the harsh reality of the first few weeks of life alone in unfamiliar surroundings and amongst total strangers can be nerve-wracking. For some, it is enough to kill the college experience altogether, causing them to drop out. Most students, anxious to show how grown-up they are and reluctant to show their true vulnerability, will never tell their parents quite how nerve-wracking the first few weeks of college are.

Much literature and information is sent home from school during the final year of your student's high school journey, most of it addressing things like college deadlines, SAT locations, and graduation requirements. Not much of the information addresses how you should prepare your student for a smooth transition from a nurtured environment among friends they have probably known since kindergarten to a place where there may be 100 or more students in a class and a professor who is a distant figure at the bottom of a huge lecture hall.

Senioritis

Sometime soon after the start of senior year, students begin to get a sense of their impending adulthood. Teachers start to treat them differently. Secure in the knowledge that students are set in their ways by the time they get this far, and the school has its best with them, teachers of seniors begin to let go. They are less rigorous regarding discipline. Students either get it or they do not at this point. Some students have matured and can handle an adult relationship with their teachers. Others still have some way to go, but all this being treated like an adult goes to their head and senioritis sets in.

Senioritis is the name of the "disease" that some high school teachers attribute to seniors. The symptoms are a general malaise, lack of caring, resistance to authority figures, and a sense of one's own impending freedom. It can be likened to working the last two weeks at work after you have given notice. You take risks and liberties that otherwise you would not. After all, what are they going to do, fire you?

College-bound seniors usually know early on in the academic year which colleges have accepted them and have often made an acceptance decision by January or

February. All that is left is to glide to the finish line, putting in just enough effort to maintain their GPA and qualify for a scholarship. For some, it is not even that important how they do on final exams.

I learned about senioritis the hard way, when my son acquired a bad case of it. I know this because he told me. One day in his senior year, he brought home a C in French. French was one of the few subjects in which he had consistently scored As and Bs throughout high school. When I asked him why he got a C in his best subject, he told me that it was due to his senioritis. I asked him what senioritis was.

"It's when you just don't care any more.
It's apathy. I have a bad case of it."

I asked him how he knows he has it.

"My science teacher told me. All kids get
it in senior year."

Sure enough, the next day I got an e-mail from his science teacher telling me that my son had a bad case of senioritis and was acting out in class.

The message that the student's get from their teachers is that this senioritis condition is normal and even that it is somehow cool to slack off during senior year. Teachers acknowledge that their growing up moves them outside of their control, and so they metaphorically throw their hands up. However, while this is safe and even harmless in high school, once students get to college they will not find such a tolerant atmosphere toward goofing off and giving up. In high school, senioritis is rewarded with your senior prom, graduation, and a great party at the end of final exams. In college, apathy and slacking off get no such reward.

The truth is most of the help that parents and students receive from their high school is focused on getting into college, not on surviving the experience. Sometime during senior year, many students will turn 18 and we will congratulate our sons and daughters on becoming adults. Then we promptly send them away from home. As your child wades through the multitude of things that need to be done during that last year of high school, and you assist him or her by taking the strain wherever you can, here are some things your child is not learning before he or she leaves home:

- **Managing money:** How to live on a budget; figuring out how much money you have and how much you should spend each week. How to write a check, or use an ATM card. Doing online banking. How to transfer funds between a home account and an out-of-state account. (The first time my son did this it did not go through properly so he did it again. The money was transferred twice and he went into overdraft.)

- **E-mail etiquette:** How to address a college professor with a Ph.D. and ask a (polite) question about class requirements. How to find his or her e-mail address. How to contact housing about changing a roommate, reporting a theft, fixing a leaky faucet, or applying for an assistant's position.

- **How to use a college "Facebook":** Computer literate students now have the edge over those who do not like to use the computer because an online "Facebook" is becoming the way to make initial contact and stay in touch with other students. Despite the fact that adults think most children are whizz-kids at computers, some are not comfortable with computers and do not like using them.

- **How to read a college catalog and determine what core classes, electives, and prerequisites are needed:** How to make changes to a schedule. Whether a certain professor can be chosen or not. What options there are if the classes think needed are full.

- **Dining alone:** Whether to, when to, and what to do if you do not feel like walking across campus in the rain to a lonely dining hall that is offering the same food as yesterday.

- **How to deal with a medical issue, such as the onset of a rash, a knee injury, or a serious cut:** When to get medical help and how to use medical insurance; how to self-medicate with over-the-counter drugs, bandages, or a knee brace. Is your child equipped with enough knowledge to know whether to take themselves to the medical center for an X-ray?

- **Reading a map, consulting a bus or train schedule, or using MapQuest and Google to figure out how to get to the nearest bank, post office, department store, grocery store, and so on:** Just because your child is on campus in a cozy dorm room and has the seven-day meal plan does not mean they will not have needs that occasionally cause them to seek resources off-campus.

- **Being a small fish in a big pond (going away to college is not the same as the first day of middle school or the first day of high school):** At the end of the high school day, your child was able to go home, sit down to a family dinner, ask you to pick up school supplies at the store, and sleep in his or her own bed. It is completely different when they go back to a strange, hard bed in a room they share with a stranger and have to walk across campus to eat.

You may see your child experiencing a great deal of freedom in senior year, coming and going between classes, enjoying multiple free periods, and so on. This may lead you to think senior year of high school is preparing your student for college life, but that is probably not true. Emotional independence and general life skills are not taught in school. Moreover, the style of academic learning your child is developing in high school is not necessarily setting them up for success in college.

The Learning Environment

The expectations, lessons, and learning environment are all quite different at the college level. Even if your child took honors classes or college-level classes in high school, the atmosphere on a college campus is so very different that the academic content of classes is only a small part of the overall environment.

Consider the contrast between taking multiple classes, back to back, for six hours a day versus a schedule in which there may be early morning and late evening classes every other day, with large periods in between when nothing is scheduled. Some of their classes can have between 100 and 200 students. It may be that they never sit next to the same person twice. Even if they know the name of the professor, the professor may never get to know your son or daughter by name and may have no idea whether they have done their homework, or whether they are even in class on a given day. There are rarely opportunities for make-ups when assignments are missed or forgotten or when illness gets in the way.

In college, homework assignments can be long and require much research, and even though homework topics may be only minimally addressed in class, they can magically appear on final exams worth a large percentage of the grade. Many professors in college have multiple tasks and duties beyond teaching, and they may use teaching assistants and senior students to grade papers and prepare lecture notes. In high school, students do a lot of work that requires memorization of dates, names, formulas, and theories. In college, the focus is more on understanding concepts, proving theories, formulating and supporting opinions, and demonstrating intellectual maturity.

In high school, there are rules, and if you break them, you are punished. In college, as in life, you may be only vaguely aware of the rules, and you may run into ethical dilemmas. No one is watching you if you goof off, break the rules, get yourself into trouble, or spend days alone in your room without talking to a soul.

In short, high school, even senior year, is not really preparing your child for life in college. There are some elements of freedom that your son or daughter is experiencing, but the overall atmosphere, both at school and at home, is still one in which your blossoming young adult is nurtured and taken care of. You, as the parent, are still fielding all problems and sheltering your student from most of the hectic whirl of what is going on during senior year. However, before you reprimand yourself for coddling your child, remember that even though you are taking the strain, you are still setting an example for your child, and are demonstrating how to cope with multiple issues at once.

Life will get hard for your child soon enough, and getting into college is an important first step on the road to maturity, so do not feel like you have to make life any harder for your student than it already is in senior year. As long as you are not writing the application essays and doing their homework for them, there is nothing wrong with picking up the slack on the sidelines and being the responsible adult, watching the calendar for college application deadlines.

Generally speaking, high school does not equip your child with any special life skills beyond balancing sports and homework, dealing with peers, and cramming for exams. Helping your student mature into a competent adult involves so much more than sending them to high school. Managing money, for example, is not taught in school but is essential to managing one's life. Once your child turns 18, he or she will be inundated with offers for credit cards, student loans, and all kinds of other opportunities for getting deep in debt. A poor college student is especially vulnerable to these attacks. Preparing your student throughout their life by talking about credit cards, savings accounts, and budgeting will go a long way toward keeping them out of financial trouble once they strike out on their own. Learning the fundamentals of budgeting is also very helpful.

I was having a conversation about careful budgeting with Stu during the summer before he started his first year of college. He was counting his summer earnings. Our arrangement was that I would take care of his first year's tuition, room and board, and he would take care of any additional spending money he may need. We would worry about the second year after we got through the first.

"So, how do you know how much money you will need?" he innocently asked.

"Well," I began, "you start by figuring

out how much you think you will spend each week on necessities, school supplies, and entertainment. Then you add in how much you think you will spend while traveling back and forth between college and home and how much you will need over Christmas vacation, including what you plan to spend on Christmas presents for the family..."

His face dropped a little more with each item as I rattled off all the possible expenses he would have to contemplate. I could tell he had reached overload as he lost interest in the conversation and started wandering off, muttering to himself:

"Boy, this growing up stuff is hard work!"

CHAPTER 2

Choosing a College Where Your Student Will Thrive

Perhaps one of the most difficult things we do as parents is deciding when to give our children the right to make their own decisions. This is especially difficult when they have reached, or are approaching, the age of majority and they have their own dreams and ideas. Whether your student was pro-active in selecting a shortlist of colleges or took the lead from you regarding which colleges to apply to, he or she eventually is faced with having to make a decision, and you are faced with the challenge of whether to influence that decision.

It may be that your student only ended up with one offer, in which case the choice is pretty easy, but many students end up with more than one, which means you have to give some thought to what goes into making the best choice, in addition to the academic record of the college. Your first thought may be to choose the best financial deal, while your student is more likely to be making a decision straight from the gut, influenced by a great night on campus during a recent visit.

Our job as parents is not to choose for them, but to help guide them in the process of making their own choice.

We can talk over the pros and cons for each college and listen carefully to their reasoning, while prompting them to consider things they may not be. We may want our children to go to the college that we went to, or that we wished we had been able to attend. We may want them to stay close to home to save money, to keep our eye on them, or because we think they are not ready to be independent.

If your student has more than one offer to choose from, there are essentially three elements to the decision: academic record, cost, and campus culture.

Campus culture is perhaps the hardest to figure out, even after a campus visit. You can narrow your choices of what kind of place you think you are going to like but there is no way to know for sure if a place is going to suit you until you experience it. Plenty of students switch to their second-choice school after spending their freshman year in their first-choice school, but then again, the vast majority of students graduate from the first college they attend. So there is no reason to spend too much time worrying about it.

There is so much more to campus life than the academic record of the college. After all, your son or daughter is going to spend the next four years there, and it will probably be their first experience living alone, not only on campus but also in town, around the city streets, and among the people of the region. Your student is not just going to school in this city; they are going to be living there for the greater part of the next four years.

An independent child raised in a bustling East Coast city may be bored to death on a small, Midwestern campus, no matter how good the scholarship and no matter how good a reputation that college has in your child's major. The reverse is also true. A student with a stellar academic record from a small Midwestern town may not necessarily do well in a sophisticated East Coast school, even if they are accepted. A sheltered student from a small town can be overwhelmed by the Ivy League campus culture, and they may have trouble fitting in. You should think carefully about where your child will thrive emotionally, not just where they will get accepted academically. This is not to say that a student should only go to school close to home, or that students from the Midwest should not attend East Coast schools. On the contrary, some students do well in environments that are completely different from what they are used to. Nevertheless, it is worth considering these things and reminding your student to think about where they will feel most comfortable.

There are other considerations too, such as ratio of boys to girls. Some technical colleges, such as Georgia Institute of Technology and Colorado School of Mines have a ratio of almost three boys to one girl. Even if your student has taken little interest in the opposite sex during the last couple of years of high school, that is going to change over the next four years. If there is a high ratio of boys to girls, or the other way around, there are sometimes neighboring schools, or groups of colleges, that are located close to each other and share social activities. If this is not the case, it could be a long, lonely college career for your student, even if the educational curriculum is outstanding.

Choosing a College Close to Home

There are some valid reasons why a student should go to college close to home. For one thing, it will be cheaper, even if it is a private college with high tuition fees. You are likely to get better scholarship and grant opportunities by going to a college in your home state. Many states pay stipends for students to go to a public college in their home state.

Most colleges, both public and private, require freshmen to live on campus for their first year. So you may not save on room and board during the first year, but you can save money on travel — your child can come home on weekends, for family get-togethers, special occasions, and, of course, for the holidays. This can be a great benefit for a student who is not ready to be fully independent.

However, there is a big difference between going to a college close to home and going to college while still living at home.

For most students, a big part of a college education is the growing up experience — learning to handle independence, living among peers, and experiencing the student lifestyle. Living on a shoestring and eating dry ramen straight from the bag for dinner is as much a rite of passage as walking across the stage to pick up a college diploma.

Beware of trying to convince your student to stay close to home because you want them close, rather than because they want to be close.

If your student wants to live at home, and you can afford for them to go away to college, you should make it clear that they are always welcome at home for visits, but they will be better off living on-campus or they will risk missing out on most of the college social life.

Most students will want to move out. This is normal and natural, and you should not take offense.

Choosing a College within Driving Distance (One Day or Less)

Perhaps the best arrangement for many students is attending a college that is within half a day's driving distance. A three or four hour drive to and from college means the family can be in easy reach and the occasional weekend at home is possible, but it is only worth making the drive if circumstances warrant. In other words, your student cannot pop home for every little thing, but in the first few weeks, when the going gets tough, they can make a trip home for a quick pick-me-up.

If the college is more than a few hours away, then the chances are high that once you say goodbye to them, you are not going to see them again until Thanksgiving, unless you can afford to travel out for the family day most colleges hold during September or October.

Choosing a College Far From Home

Some 18-year-olds are ready to move away from home, some think they are, and some are just not ready and they know it. Several motivating factors may determine whether your student wants to attend school in a distant part of the country. Our family has several acquaintances that chose the University of Puget Sound at various times for various reasons. Since we live in Colorado, Oregon is quite a trek. The daughter of one of my friends chose to go there because she did a lot of research into the school and the weather in the area, and she thought that the cool, rainy climate would really suit her. Another friend's son chose the University of Seattle because he is interested in music, and there is a certain music culture in Seattle that he felt would suit him. Another girl chose a small, East Coast school because of the small classroom size along with the small, friendly community atmosphere, and it offered the highly specialized major she was looking for (Japanese).

Stu chose Atlanta because of the school's prestige in his engineering discipline and because, after the overnight campus visit, he was taken with the atmosphere of the place and knew he would enjoy the campus culture. I encouraged him to accept, because Atlanta offers an internationally recognized cooperative program that would allow Stu to work and earn part of his college tuition. Ian chose Nebraska because he was a National Merit Scholar and Nebraska offered him a full academic scholarship. Because he wants to become a doctor and will have eight college years to fund, he knew this was a solid financial move.

No matter the reason, the logistics of attending a school far from home have their own little complications, but it is not all bad. For Stu, we have to worry about the price of plane tickets, trying to plan ahead, and keeping our eye out for bargain airfares, whereas Ian just has to hop in the car and can come and go with little notice. He also has a reasonably direct Greyhound Bus route when his car is not working. However, it is worth noting that Stu's journey, since he comes by plane, is actually much shorter than Ian's. Ian spends 10 hours in the car, or 12 hours on the bus, but Stu only has a three-hour plane ride, and his whole journey is under six hours door-to-door. If you or your spouse travel a lot with your jobs and rack up frequent flier miles, it can actually be more economical than you think to opt for a short plane ride over a long car journey.

If you do not have the benefit of frequent flier miles and your student attends school far from home, you have to worry about things like whether or not they can afford to come home for shorter visits, like Thanksgiving, Fall Break (which is usually only two or three days long), and Spring Break. If you have enough money to fly them home for short breaks, (or if they have enough) then it probably does not matter where they choose to go, but if finding the money to buy airplane tickets will be a problem, your student has more to think about.

As a parent, you will have to worry about what to do if your student gets sick, including homesick, which can be very real and very dramatic. Your student, of course, will not think about this possibility when selecting a college, but it may hit them harder than they think several weeks after they have gone off to college and have moved into the dorm.

Traveling Back and Forth for Visits

There is a day or weekend when parents are invited to visit the college for "Parents' Day." Whether your student is near or far, you will have to decide whether you want to go to campus. If you have been a conscientious parent up until now and done everything with your child, you may have already spent a long summer, or even the last two summers, trekking around various campuses with your student while he or she was making up his or her mind on where to go. You have possibly attended new student orientation with your student, and you have probably just dropped him or her off at college at the start of the school year. This means you are probably aching for a vacation of your own, one that does not involve college counselors telling you how great their college is.

Financially, you may be sick of scraping every last penny together for yet another airfare or hotel bill, and are desperately in need of some time to yourself. And yet here is another college trip looming and you have to make a decision about whether or not to attend.

The reason colleges have Parents' Day a few weeks into the semester is because homesickness tends to peak around that time. Parents' Day is one strategy that many colleges have employed in an effort to decrease the freshman dropout rate. If you can stand one more trip, this is one worth making. It is an opportunity for you to see how your student is settling in and gives your student an opportunity to show you how grown-up they have become. After you leave, they will have a renewed sense of being able to stand on their own two feet.

Unless you have other travel plans that take you to the area, it probably is not necessary to visit them otherwise. It is important to bring them home, if you can, for that first Thanksgiving in freshman year, and for Christmas and Spring Break, so you should factor the cost of travel into the budget and make sure you can afford that before you commit as a family to a long distance college. However, after the first year, you will notice a dwindling in the number of times they need to come home, and they will become much more resourceful on their own. So as time goes by, the need to come up with so many travel funds will subside as your resourceful student finds other things to do during their college breaks.

Getting There and Back with Luggage

If you choose a school that is not within driving distance, the biggest logistics problem you face is what to do about luggage. Stu picked a school far from home. He is a cellist and intended to participate in the Georgia Tech Orchestra. The cello is a large instrument, and getting it to Georgia by plane presented quite a challenge.

His acceptance meant we would need to consider:

- Whether we should fly him out or take him out by car (which meant four days on the road, including hotel bills and road food).

- How to cart everything out there if we went by plane, including the cello, which is both large and delicate.

- Whether or not he would be able to fulfill his childhood dream of owning a dorm room fridge because transporting it would be a huge problem.

We decided to travel to Georgia by plane. Stu had traveled by plane several times with the cello and it was not simple. You have to go to security and ensure that they scan it on the X-ray machine without damaging it. Then they convey it to the special handling section. When you arrive, you have to figure out where to pick it up because it cannot be placed on the regular luggage-claim conveyer belt.

Getting out there was not the problem because I would go with him and help him carry things, but getting back was a problem. I was worried that he would not be able to manage the cello and his other luggage by himself. I also worried that he would be preoccupied with exams up to the last day of the semester and not have time to worry about shipping his luggage back.

The issue of how to get Stu, his cello, and a year's worth of supplies out to Georgia was a big deal to me. I stressed over it most of the summer after he had made his decision to accept the offer.

In exasperation, I called the residence counselors at Tech and asked them what they recommended. Most students took two big suitcases with as much as they could cram in them, paid the excess baggage, and got on with life. That would have worked if it had not been for the cello.

One day I received a flyer in the mail. It was actually addressed to my other son, Ian, who was already attending college. It advertised, "We ship door to dorm." I thought this could be the answer. The shipping company called "MadPackers" advertised that they dealt primarily with college students. They would deliver boxes and packing materials to our home, arrange pick up of the boxes, and deliver them to the dorm room on a specified day. At the end of the semester, they would do the exact same thing in reverse, including delivering empty boxes to the dorm room, picking them up and transporting them to our home. They would deliver microwaves, dorm fridges, electronic equipment, and books; they even offered a wardrobe box.

This seemed too good to be true.

I went to the MadPackers Web site and made the arrangements. The boxes were going to picked up from our home and delivered to Atlanta the day after we were due to arrive.

On the designated morning in Atlanta, despite 100 degree heat, Stu and I waited patiently at the designated street corner during the delivery window. About one hour into the time window, I received a call from the local delivery courier. They wanted to know how many boxes I was expecting. We had shipped four boxes. Two had arrived.

Of the two that arrived, one had a few food supplies, and

the other was bedding. We had lost most of his clothes and toiletries, all the supplies he needed to start college (calculator, pens, notebooks), and his new dorm room refrigerator.

Words cannot explain how I felt. I had invested the entire last year of my life in helping Stu get into and travel to college. I had stressed for months over how to get his cello and his luggage out there. The next day, I was due to catch a plane back to Colorado and would have to leave my son all alone in a strange city, with no friends, no relatives, no transport, none of his personal items, none of his school supplies, and none of his clothes.

Before I left Atlanta, I bought Stu a few clothes "to tide him over until the boxes arrived."

MadPackers eventually delivered the third of the four boxes, right after that they went bankrupt. One full month into the first semester, Stu received the new clothes we had bought him for college. We finally located the last box in a lost and found warehouse. Two months after my son started college, he received the last of his belongings and was finally able to consider himself settled in.

In retrospect, the fridge and multiple other items could have been purchased in Atlanta. It would have been cheaper to purchase bed linens, towels, and underwear locally, and literally throw them away at the end of the semester, rather than to invest in a costly shipping arrangement that took my money, lost his belongings, and went out of business.

As parents, we try and do our best to send our children

out into the world with everything they need, and our first inclination is to set everything up for them before they leave home. I learned the hard way that this is not necessarily the best approach. It would have been easier and cheaper to buy most things locally than going through months of making do without the right supplies.

For most people, the best arrangement is probably to go with the excess baggage solution, but if your child has something awkward to ship, like a cello, consider buying other things after you arrive.

My friend Janet's son graduated from Georgia Tech the year before Stu started there. I called and asked her how her son managed with transporting his belongings. Janet and her son had family in the area, so he was able to leave things like his dorm refrigerator with relatives. If you do not have relatives in the area, you simply have to learn to travel light and use local storage facilities over the summer. Janet said they bought many things after they arrived, so they did not have to carry them. With the cost of shipping items, it can actually be just as cheap to buy many things once you arrive and dispose of them before you come home, sell them, or give them away.

Choosing Between a Small or Large Campus

We hear that small campuses offer small and friendly classes with lots of personal attention, while large campuses have huge auditoriums that hold a hundred or more students and the professor never knows anyone by name. But there is a lot more to it, and you cannot always judge how your student will like one or the other.

Stu is a sociable boy and likes to be personal with his teachers. I thought he would enjoy the close personal touch of a smaller campus. He was recruited by the University of Tulsa and they offered mechanical engineering and music, his two degree choices, so we put it on our list of places to visit and apply to. Stu was so impressed by all he read about Tulsa that, before we went there, it was absolutely his top pick. He liked it more than Georgia Tech, which he was not interested in at first because they did not offer a major in music. He also liked it more than Colorado State, which not only offered both his subjects but also, being nestled in prime ski country, offered easy access to the great outdoors, which Stu loved. However, from the first minute that we arrived in Tulsa for the campus tour, he knew it was not the place for him. His initial comment after I parked the car and started walking to the Student Union to find the tour was:

"My high school is bigger than this place!"

The University of Tulsa is a good institution. We were both impressed by the level of education, the high quality of teaching, offered, and the respectful and straightforward way that students handled themselves on campus. If the small-town atmosphere is going to work well for your student, this could be a good pick. But it did not work for Stu.

If your student is trying to decide between colleges, I absolutely recommend the campus visit. It can make a big difference when you see and feel the place, versus reading about it in the catalog and on the Web site.

Georgia, which had none of the attributes Stu was looking for on paper, ended up being his number one pick because he was drawn to the culture of the place and felt like it was somewhere he would fit in. Yet I never would have expected him to choose it because it is very large, in a big city, and far from home. So far, he does not regret his choice. After spending his first year, despite getting off to a rocky start, he still enjoys Tech and does not regret his choice.

CHAPTER 3

Attending Freshman Orientation

In addition to setting aside our life savings to get our children though four years of college, and the 50 to 75 dollar application fee that accompanies most college applications, we also have to decide whether to invest thousands of dollars per trip to visit the short-listed colleges and later, after acceptance, freshman orientation. In addition, many colleges offer some kind of summer bonding experience for freshmen where they are invited to spend a week on a deep-sea fishing trip to Alaska, or some equally scintillating experience of a lifetime.

To get your student into one college, here is a summary of the possible trips that you will have to consider taking:

- Pre-attendance campus tour

- Post-acceptance, pre-attendance bonding experience trip

- Freshman orientation

- Parents' Weekend (usually during the first semester)

- Move-in weekend

If you are looking colleges far from home, then you have to take into account airfare, hotels, car rental, road food, and miscellaneous spending. You can figure on an average of a couple of thousand dollars for you and your student for each of these trips. That means you could end up easily being $10,000 into your college savings account before you even pay a dime toward college tuition fees. So it is worth researching each of these trips and deciding whether you want to go on them or not.

Campus Tours

College counselors recommend applying for somewhere between two and six colleges. Each application requires an application fee of 35 to 75 dollars, so the number you apply to may be limited by the number of application fees you are prepared to pay. However, six colleges is quite a large number to decide among if you are planning to visit them all.

Everyone should have at least one local college in their short list, and, even if you do not, it is a good idea to visit a couple of local campuses. This gives your student a relatively cheap look at some campuses to serve as a basis for comparison. The number you visit after that depends on your financial situation. Obviously if you apply to six colleges, the best of all worlds is to visit those six. But this can be financially draining. Some parents choose to save the campus visits until after acceptance because there is not much point in visiting a campus where your son or daughter is not accepted. There are arguments for and against this. Some people think the campus visit ensures acceptance. While most colleges assure you in writing that a visit is not necessary for acceptance, there may be a grain of truth to the fact that the more times you get your son or daughter's name in front of the admissions counselors, the greater their chances are of being accepted. A campus visit prior to acceptance does demonstrate a certain amount of commitment and genuine interest, and colleges know this.

In our family, Ian's college choice was a financial one. He wanted to accept the best scholarship offer and financial deal. Nebraska had offered Ian a full four-year academic scholarship. For this reason, he thought that visiting campuses was not essential. I had little or no money to spare at that point.

I had three college careers to pay for ahead of me, and so, as my first son embarked on his college career, I was cautious about spending money on superfluous trips. I do not think I appreciated at that point the importance of campus visits in the decision-making process. Later, after I had made three campus visits with Stu and witnessed his reaction to each of the colleges, I deeply regretted not making the financial effort with Ian to take him to some of his college picks. However, the University of Nebraska turned out to be a great school for Ian, and he is happy with his decision.

In Stu's case, my decision to make some visits was based solely on the fact that Stu had no clue what kind of college he wanted to go to or what he wanted to major in. At the time, he was torn between electrical engineering and music. The first campus we visited was Colorado State in Fort Collins, only a three-hour drive from where we lived. Colorado State is a beautiful campus in the Colorado wilderness close to ski country.

We attended a presentation given by the School of Engineering. The first thing Stu learned was that Colorado State supported a double major option and both engineering and music were offered as majors. He looked at me excitedly.

> *"I won't have to choose between them! I can do both here!"*

The engineering professor went on to tell us about a race car they had built in the School of Engineering. After sitting through several presentations already, Stu had begun to drift off, but his ears pricked up when they talked about the race car. They described how they had worked on it as a class project, and won a place of distinction in a national competition.

> *"What engineering discipline were they talking about?" his interest was keenly awakened.*

> *"Mechanical engineering."*

> *"Then that's what I want to do. A double major with music and mechanical engineering. Right. That's that then. It's all settled."*

And so the Colorado State campus visit was key in helping

Stu understand what is out there and what is interesting to him. After that trip, he never waivered about wanting to do mechanical engineering. I highly recommend campus visits, at least local ones, for students who are undecided about what they want to do. Take them to several presentations in contrasting subjects and see what catches their attention.

His choice of major was further reinforced after his stay in a fraternity house at Georgia Institute of Technology (where music was only offered as a minor). After Stu came back from Atlanta, he was absolutely adamant about going to Tech and would not hear of going anywhere else, even after he obtained a substantial scholarship for music at Tulane.

Later, we talked about the offers he received and the options he had available to him.

> *"I can't imagine agreeing to go anywhere*
> *that I haven't even seen," he told me.*

The University of Tulsa had been his first pick until he went there and saw it. Tulsa is a wonderful campus, and the students are very warm and friendly, but it is a small campus and that did not suit Stu.

Ian, on the other hand, had assured me early in the game that it made no difference whether we visited the campus or not because he was "making a purely financial decision."

For Ian, it was only important to dig as little as possible into his personal resources the first four years so he would have something left to pay for the second four years of his medical degree. His brother will be embarking on his undergraduate degree around the time he graduates from Nebraska. In fact, there will be one crossover year where all three of my boys will be in college at the same time. (I have not even tried to figure out how I will manage that.) But Ian will have a second chance at choosing a campus for his post-graduate degree. I have promised him we will visit any two or three colleges of his choosing when the time comes.

Ian is enjoying life at Nebraska University. It is a great college with an excellent reputation in one of the nicest towns in Nebraska. He was lucky. However, in retrospect, I shortchanged him out of a valuable experience, and if I had the chance to do it over again I would take him on some college tours.

Freshman Orientation

I strongly recommend for both parents and students to attend freshman orientation. Freshman orientation usually consists of a two to three day stay on campus that takes place a few weeks prior to the start of the first semester. It allows students to familiarize themselves with the campus, choose their classes, and meet their fellow freshmen. Most colleges also offer something for parents at this time, with a special agenda including a campus tour, the opportunity to eat in the dining hall, and a chance to visit your student's residence hall. Most colleges separate the students and parents for most of the orientation, and they entice students with the sweet smell of fraternity parties and rush week while entertaining parents with the more mundane details of when the student bill is due and how to pay it online.

So why should you go? Well, for one thing, if you do not, your child will feel like the only student in the entire freshman year whose parents did not show up to collect them at the end of orientation. Students get to try two days of college life away from their parents, and at the end they are pumped to the core that they survived two days on campus alone. They emerge victoriously, waiving their first class schedule in the air, just dying to tell someone how excited they are about starting college. After 18 years of rejoicing all their first times — their first tooth, their first step, kindergarten, middle school, and high school, all culminating in high school graduation and their first college acceptance — ask yourself, do you want to miss this day?

The number of opportunities you will have to be with your child, and share in their triumphs and disasters, rapidly diminishes from this point forward. This is like a last chance.

It is also a good opportunity to explore the campus and become familiar with your student's new surroundings, their new home away from home. It will give you an understanding of how tiny their dorm room is, what kinds of things they will need to bring, and what they will not have room for. It will clue you in on the weather you should expect in the region if it is not close to home, and what kinds of clothes they should bring.

Perhaps the most important thing about the orientation for parents is the opportunity to meet other parents. As high school seniors, and now young adults, our children exhibit an array of frustrating behaviors. They pull away and treat us badly; they act remorseful for a moment, and then misbehave even worse than they did before. They yell and scream at us and take out their frustrations on us, and then they cling to us or lock us out when life gets them down. They appear so grown-up one minute, and then we find them crawling around the basement floor playing with their Legos the next, just as they did when they were five.

Meeting with other parents can be comforting. Hearing that other parents are experiencing similar things helps us appreciate the fact that this is a stage in our child's life, and not their new grown-up personality. Hearing that Jenny from Tennessee wanted to pick the college that her boyfriend was going to, or that Jeremy from Baltimore refuses to entertain the idea of buying anything other than jeans and T-shirts for his college wardrobe, assures us our children are normal and their behavior is normal.

Pre-Orientation Field Trips

Some colleges offer pre-college bonding experiences. These trips are usually a week or so long, and they often involve an exciting experience, such as camping in the wilderness, white-water rafting, a trip to Europe, or something equally exotic. They often cost several thousand dollars. If you and your student have the money, and you are willing to spend it on this type of activity, there are some advantages.

It is another opportunity for them to stretch their wings, get out on their own, and meet other freshmen who will be attending their college. Of course, there is no guarantee they will run into any of the same students once they start college. Nonetheless, if your student has not taken many field trips up until now, it could result in a positive experience and be something your child will always remember.

It is not necessary, however. There will be plenty of other students who will not have participated in the trip. In fact, the vast majority of the freshmen population do not go on these trips. That may be for financial reasons; however, money is not the only negative. For some students and parents alike, it is yet another pressure point that threatens to break the family apart during their last summer together, adding to the stress of preparations. You may to have to buy special clothes for the trip and arrange to drop off and pick up your student at some distant point of departure and arrival, or fly them out to it.

Even if you can afford this sort of trip, you may find your student is quite reluctant. His or her stomach is already churning at the thought of leaving home, being among strangers, and making his or her own way in life. He or she may see this, even though it sounds like an exciting adventure, as just one more thing to cope with. He of she really wants to spend this summer visiting with high school friends, hanging out in familiar haunts while there is still the opportunity, and spending some quiet time alone under his or her headphones mentally preparing for the year ahead.

Early Starts for Athletes

If your child is going to be participating in an athletic program, it may be necessary to start college earlier than the majority of freshmen. Your student may be nervous about not starting at the same time as everyone else. In reality, an early start for athletic programs usually gives students an enormous edge.

Not only will they be more familiar with the campus before the start of classes, but also the athletic team experience encourages strong friendships that endure throughout the college years and beyond. An early start will fill your student with the confidence that they can survive and succeed alone before the rest of the college students even arrive.

If you have an early start, summer will be a short, whirlwind experience for you and your student, and you may want to think about a visit right before the start of school, or during parent weekend, which is most often held in September.

CHAPTER 4

Planning Finances and Health Insurance

There are two over-arching ideas relating to your student and their finances. The first relates to the practical issue of ensuring your student has access to money when it is needed, and the second relates to the more philosophical idea of whether your student knows how to be responsible with money. Underlying the second idea is the question of exactly how much money will they need and who will supply it — you or them?

Let us start with the practical aspects of how to store and access the money and work our way up to the much harder discussion of who pays for what.

Access to Your Student's Records

The Family Educational Rights and Privacy Act (FERPA) is a federal law designed to protect your student's rights. While your student is a minor, the law gives you, the parent, certain rights with respect to your student's educational records. You have the right to inspect your student's records and request corrections. You also have to give permission for the records to be released.

Once your student turns 18, these rights are transferred from you to your student.

That means you are no longer eligible to view your student's records unless given written permission to do so. By law, the college must respect your student's decision. This means you may never know what grades they are getting (what they tell you, with all due respect to your student, may not be 100 percent accurate).

Therefore, you may or may not end up being able to view your student's academic records or accounts. Even though you may be the one paying the bill, that does not give you the automatic right to see it.

Of course, you have the right to tell your student, "No access, no money." That is between you and your student. You cannot fight this point with the college, because they have to uphold the law. You need to iron it out as a private matter.

Money Management

Do you have a spender or a saver? Most people fall into one of these two categories. If you have a saver, you probably do not have to worry much. Savers tend to be frugal and are intuitively good at budgeting and organizing their money. Spenders are often generous people, but tend to be less organized when it comes to understanding the value of things and how to budget.

Good money-management skills are not something your student will acquire in three short months over the summer prior to departure. Some parents give their children responsibility for money at an early age, while others keep a tight hold on the financial reins while their children are minors. The more practice your student has at managing their own money, the better off they will be on their own. It is a good idea to start giving your student increasing responsibility for his or her money throughout high school. If they have had some experience with earning money, then hopefully you helped them set up a bank account for their earnings and they know how to use it.

Many of us are fully automated and online now when it comes to money. It is not unusual for students not to understand things like how to deposit a live check in their account. When I pay Ian's bill at Nebraska, the bill usually comes in and requires payment before all the scholarship funds kick in. UNL's policy is to send a refund to Ian, regardless of who pays the bill. The first time he received the refund, he had no idea what it was for and did not understand the concept that it was a live check. He has always been good at looking after his own money, but he was oblivious to the concept of his tuition bill and his scholarship funds, since he gave me permission to do all that online on his behalf. He kept the check for about two weeks before he said anything about it to us. He thought it may be junk mail, one of those fake checks trying to get you to take out a student loan. Luckily we found out about the check and were able to deposit it back into our account. Every little bit extra counts when you are paying out large sums of money on a regular basis.

In their first year of college, some students accumulate quite a bit of cash — from graduation gifts, savings from summer jobs, generous grandparents, and so on. If this is the case, depending on your financial arrangement with your student, they may end up with more than they intend to spend for the first year. It is a good idea to work with your student to help them understand the value of a savings account or Certificate of Deposit (CD). That way, they stand less of a chance to overspend, and even a small amount of interest can seem like a good deal to a poor student.

Many online savings accounts are currently paying better interest rates than CDs. These accounts are easy to access; it takes about three days to transfer money in or out of an online savings account, and you can transfer it directly into your checking account. That way, if they do overspend, they have access to more of their own cash, but it is not in the primary money pool, so it is somewhat protected. A CD locks the money up for the term you select — usually six months or one year. If you have a serious spender to contend with, this may be a good thing, and worth considering.

When you are calculating how much the whole college package is going to cost, there are many miscellaneous expenses that are easy to overlook. When you are preparing your college budget, these are some of the most common expenses your student will have:

- Tuition — including lab fees and materials

- Books

- Room and Board (meal plan and dorm room)

- Health Insurance, if needed

- Fraternity fees, if any

- Parking fees, if taking a car

- Storage fees for a musical instrument or sports equipment, if any

- Entertainment — such as football tickets, recreation center fees, theater, and others

- Miscellaneous expenses and weekly spending money

Spending Money

How much spending money does a student need? This is a difficult question to answer because everyone is so different. It also depends on whether you are in a big, expensive city or small town in Middle America, and whether your student needs to consider expenses such as public transport, or gas and insurance for their car. Girls may spend more than boys, because they buy things like cosmetics and usually like to have more clothes, accessories, and so on. People who are social and go out a lot spend more on entertainment than a highly academic individual who stays close to the dorm room.

College estimates of student spending money range from about $800 per year to over $2000. So reality is probably somewhere in between, and it may be a question of how much your student can raise, rather than how much should be made available.

If you are paying tuition for your son or daughter to attend college, or partial tuition if they have received a scholarship, it is reasonable to expect them to come up with their own spending money for the academic year, either through working on campus during the school year, or by saving money from summer jobs. In fact, some college financial packages include a work opportunity for students in need.

If your student chose an in-state school and has the benefit of scholarships, stipends, and grants, then you may be one of the lucky parents who can afford to provide spending money for your student. The cost of room and board alone can be enough to stretch your budget. If you are also faced with out-of-state tuition bills, you may not have enough money to provide spending money as well.

Student Cards

Most colleges offer their own student card, which is essentially a debit card. In most cases, the student card will be a campus ID card used for everything from gaining access to dorms and dining halls to paying for books, laundry, and soda from vending machines. The student simply swipes the card and the amount is debited from their student card account. These cards usually work on campus, and they are often honored at local vendors, such as restaurants and coffee shops that are frequented by students.

These cards will all be a little different, depending on the college, but in general they cannot be used to obtain cash. You will also need to find out whether the college allows the student to build up debt on the card once the funds expire. If they build up debt, the amount is added to the college bill and becomes payable on the college billing schedule. This is a handy solution because your student can do everything with just one card. However, it does restrict students to places that accept the card.

Because you will, by law, not be given access to your student's records, unless your student grants you access you will not know how much money they have on the card. If you think money management will be a problem for your student and you want more control (which is only advisable if it is actually your money as opposed to your student's money), then a joint bank account and ATM card will let you monitor spending through the bank's online services.

Bank Accounts

Even if your student plans to make heavy use of the student ID card as a way to access funds, it is a good idea for them to have their own bank account. Once a student turns 18, they can get their own account and you do not have to be a co-signer. If they have their own funds from after-school or summer jobs, gifts from relatives, savings, and scholarships, it is a good idea to let them have their independence.

If they already have a bank account, you will want to check and make sure there is an ATM on campus or nearby where they can access their money, and if the bank is even represented in the state where they are going to school. Some banks will have ATM access in states where they are not physically represented. Make sure your student will have access without incurring additional fees by using ATMs not associated with the bank where their money is held. Incurring a two or three dollar fee every time you get out a twenty-dollar bill quickly puts a strain on a college student's budget.

It may be necessary for them to open up a local bank account. Stu maintains two bank accounts, one in Colorado and one in Georgia. With online access, he is able to transfer money back and forth between them so he can have access to his cash both when he is at school and when he comes home, without incurring additional fees for out-of-state withdrawals. I should probably mention that neither bank account has much money in it, but he watches the balance so it does not get too low.

Most banks are fairly lenient with students and do not require a minimum balance, but you still want to make sure you teach your student how to avoid overdraft fees by tying the account to an overdraft protection mechanism, such as a savings account, or maintaining a "liner" of a few hundred dollars that essentially represents "non-spending" money.

ATM Cards

This is probably going to be your student's primary

access to cash. The key thing is to research what banks are supported by the ATMs on campus without incurring additional fees, and then you should make sure your student has an account at one of those banks. Small campuses may only be supported by one bank's ATM machines. If your student does not already have an ATM card, it may be a good idea to teach her how to use one before she leaves. This is not because it is hard, but when everything is new to you, it is nice to know as many things in advance as possible. It just helps build confidence to have some things you know how to do when you get there. Especially things like getting money.

Do not forget to make sure your student understands that even though electronic banking uses real-time transactions, ATM transactions can sometimes take a day or two to show up. ATM purchases occur as placeholders in your account, and may appear as "pending" transactions until the vendor completes their accounts. So even if you are checking their balance responsibly, when you are down to the last few dollars, as students often are, you need to be particularly watchful for latent ATM transactions if you want to avoid overdraft fees. The bottom line is you need to keep an independent record of how much money is in your account because it may be slightly less at any given moment than the balance that shows up online.

Credit Cards

Whether to use a credit card or not is more of a personal

philosophy. Some people use them as a convenience and pay them off every month. Other people let them build up, carry a balance, and pay the interest without even thinking about it. Paying interest on a purchase makes no sense on a student's budget.

The important thing to know is once your student turns 18, especially as a college student, the credit card companies will be after them offering amazing deals and fantastic special offers.

You may not even know if your student gets one.

I have given each of my sons a credit card "for emergencies" on one of my own credit accounts. I never carry a balance on this account so that if they do have an emergency, I will not be paying interest on it. Credit cards are handy for making online purchases. They are considered safer than ATM cards because you have certain rights with respect to transactions that go bad if they are made by credit card. You do not have the same rights when you use an ATM card for your Internet purchases. Your student should have the ability to make Internet purchases because, at the very least, they can find good deals for textbooks, and they can resell books they no longer need or want. They will get much better prices than reselling or buying used through the bookstore.

It is not a bad idea to have possession of a credit card if you treat it like a convenient payment option and not a way of purchasing things you cannot afford. I think about things like Ian running out of gas on his 10-hour drive home or getting stuck in a storm and needing to stop and stay in a motel while a storm passes, and I want him to be protected. I can also use it as a way to offer them special treats or help them pay for books. When they are feeling bad and I am feeling helpless, being able to say, "Why don't you find a nice DVD or some iTunes on the Internet and put it on my credit card!" gives me a way to reach out to them in their hour of need.

Wire Transfers

By wire transfers, I am referring to those places that you pay the money to, along with an outrageous fee, so you can get cash to someone in a distant place. To send it, your student would have to figure out where they have to go off campus to receive the money. If you get things set up properly so your student has access to cash from an ATM machine through a bank account, you should never need to do this because you should always be able to make an online transfer from your account into his or hers.

Health Insurance

If it has been a while since you checked your health insurance policy, here are some of the features you might like to check on:

- Up to what age can your dependent remain covered if they are full-time college student (ranges usually from 23 to 25)?

- What is their definition of "full-time" student,

and does your student meet it (usually 12 or more credits is considered full-time)?

- Does your insurance provider offer service out-of-state?

- If you go "out-of-network," what is your deductible and co-pay going to be?

- Does the college offer health insurance (most do), and how much is it compared to what you would have to pay for your own coverage? If you do not have a good out-of-network or out-of-state coverage, it could end up being cheaper to purchase separate health insurance.

Last, but most important, does your student know what health care coverage she has and how to use it? Or how to find an in-network provider and what the co-pay should be? Does your student know what health care services are available for "free" on-campus and what services cost money?

Learning to Budget

Whether you scratch things out on the back of a napkin or draw up a complex Excel spreadsheet, your student should not start college without having some concept of how much money is in her account(s), and how much she ought to draw out every week to get to the end of the year without running out of money.

If they are earning their spending money as they go, they

should have some kind of plan to put some aside against emergencies and not be spending every dollar, because this will leave them without any income if they choose to come home for a four-week Christmas break or just a weekend.

If they are going off to college with a fully-funded bank account, they should have some notion of how much of it they can spend in one semester, on Christmas break, and how much they should aim to come home with at the end of the year.

They do not learn this in school, and they will not learn it in college. If you have not taught it to them, they probably do not know it. If you have an undisciplined approach to money and rarely know how much money is in your account at any given time, your offspring may have an undisciplined approach, too. If you have not done anything to teach them about budgeting, do not be surprised when they call you to ask for more money, even though you sent them off to college with plenty of funds.

Paying the College Bill

For me, and for many of us, this is the hardest part of sending our children to college, and one of the biggest factors in determining where they can go.

When you start the college process, all the guidance literature tells you to worry about where you want to go and how to get in there and do not worry about the finances. With scholarships, tuitions, grants, and student loans, it will all work out in the end, they tell you confidently.

Then there is the "Roseanne" episode where the eldest daughter, who worked hard for an A grade point average, is told by her mother that there is no college fund, so the daughter elopes with her boyfriend, bitterly disappointed.

If there is no college fund, and money is an issue, be careful what you promise your student. It is true that most colleges offer some form of scholarship, but even after generous scholarships, tuition fees can still be high. "Financial Awards" usually include at least some portion of loans. A freshman student can borrow up to $3500 for the first year of college in Stafford Loans. This means every expense above $3500 (which, by the way, may not even be enough to pay for one semester room and board) not covered by scholarships and grants, will be offered to you, the parent, as a loan opportunity.

The year that Stu was looking at colleges, Tulane University in Louisiana was doing some heavy recruiting and offering to waive the application fee. It was one year after Hurricane Katrina had devastated the area, and ever mindful of the budget (Stu is my second son and started college only one year behind his brother), I thought we may find a bargain at Tulane. It had a good reputation and offered both mechanical engineering and music, the two subjects that interested Stu. We made an audition tape of Stu playing the cello and sent it off. He was accepted with generous offerings of both academic and music scholarships. But after running the calculations, and adding up room, board, travel, and so on, the final numbers for four years, even if he maintained all of his scholarships, were still out of my reach.

Ian was lucky enough to receive a generous scholarship from Denver University. As his home state, Denver would have been a nice opportunity to save some travel bills and allow Ian to have independence while being in traveling distance of home. However, after we did the math, it was still a hefty sum over four years that would leave me penniless and him with massive student loans.

So if you believe your children are destined to go to Yale or Stanford, I say let them go for it. They may get in and they need to know it or they will spend the rest of their life wondering if they could have been accepted. However, if your college fund will not cover $40,000 a year in fees, think carefully what their major is going to allow them to earn before letting them sign up for $120,000 in student loans (before interest).

It breaks my heart to hear stories of young graduates from expensive colleges going into teaching, for example, with $80,000 of student loans. The money they earn teaching is not conducive to rapidly paying down that sort of debt, which is relentlessly building interest even as they wonder where the next payment is coming from.

If you are thinking of student loans as the answer to sending your student to college, run a calculation (try **http://Kiplinger.com/tools**) on principal and interest, and figure out what the sum owed will be when your student graduates. Then make sure they understand it continues to accrue interest after they start to pay it off. Assess what type of job your student will qualify for after obtaining the degree and how much they are likely to earn in the first five years. Will it be enough to make payments on the loan? How many years do you think it is reasonable for a new graduate to spend paying down student loans? I know at least three people who have told me recently that they paid off their student loans at age 38. Everyone I talk to has a story of someone they know who is struggling to pay down student loans.

Think carefully if your student is a girl. Girls have been known to graduate expensive colleges with high student loan debts, then get married, give up their career and stay home with their children. Staying home with your children is a wonderful thing. I did it myself. But giving up your earning potential when you have debts to pay off is not smart. The best thing is not to accrue much debt to begin with.

If your child is studying for an arts degree, as opposed to an engineering degree or something else likely to generate plenty of income, and you are not in a position to offer a lot of financial support, you may want to recommend against the student loan route. A better approach will be to build up some credits at a local community college while working to save money, and transfer to a big college for junior and senior year. But beware of this approach; only a driven student will follow through and make the transition.

Books

How much books are going to cost will depend on how many credits your student is taking, where they go to college, and what their major is. Engineering, scientific, and medical books tend to be more expensive than English literature. Overall though, you are looking at somewhere between $500 and $750 per semester for the average college education, give or take a few hundred.

The first semester, it is hard to do anything other than pay up and get the books. By the second semester, your student may be able to shop around local bookstores, search bulletin boards for used books, resell books back to the bookshop, or sell them on eBay or Amazon.

Some college professors may try to help students avoid buying books by pointing them to reference notes online. Others may change their mind and substitute different books than those advertised in the syllabus, so help your student find a safe place to keep the receipt. Most bookstores will take books back if they are within a certain period of time and in new condition.

Scholarships

Some scholarships are renewable and others are not. If your student has scholarship offers you will want to check on two things:

- Is it renewable?

- What are the conditions for renewing?

There are always conditions attached to scholarships, and they are usually paid directly to the school so the money never passes through your hands. Renewable scholarships are usually dependent on grades, and they automatically renew if your student attains the appropriate grades. There may be paperwork associated with the renewal, which you or your student should keep an eye out for as the year ends.

Another thing to note about scholarships is that your student will have a tax liability if any amount of the scholarship is used for anything other than academic tuition. If the scholarship covers room and board, for example, that amount is taxable, so you should check with your tax consultant. The scholarship is always in the student's name, and together with summer earnings or part-time work, this can be enough to reach the limits set by the IRS for your student to file a tax return.

Getting a Job to Make Ends Meet

Some financial packages will offer a student a job on campus to earn enough money to reach the required expenses. If this is the case, your student may have to accept the job to meet the conditions for receiving other monies offered in the package.

If a job is not part of the financial package, your student may have to decide whether getting a part-time job (on-campus or off) makes sense in your particular financial circumstances. This can be a difficult decision because the first year of college brings so many other things to cope with that even a part-time job can increase stress and workload. No parent wants his or her child to start out under pressure.

College counselors realize the pressure that is placed on freshmen students. Some do not allow freshmen to bring cars on campus for this reason. There is a lot going on, a lot to do, and a lot to keep up with. However, if money is an issue, your student should start looking for a job on campus before they even get to college. Most college Web sites will have resources for job hunting. The big advantage of a campus job is that campus employers are tolerant of college schedules and make allowances for exam week and so on, whereas a job in town may not offer the same level of tolerance toward part-time student employees.

Once your student has been in college one full year, he will have a good idea of how he wants to earn extra money and will have access to additional job search resources on campus. Also, there are a number of opportunities during the summer and the school year to work as a research assistant.

CHAPTER 5

Things to Teach Your Children Before They Leave Home

It is sometimes hard to remember that our generation takes certain things for granted that our children never learn. For example, can your student read an analog watch? Or can they only rattle off the time in digital numbers? Because we live in a fast-paced, technological world, we are often amazed at how tech savvy our children are, but forget that it comes at the expense of learning some of the things that we, as the older generation, take for granted. Here is a list of survival skills that your child may need once you are not there to ask, and you may have forgotten to teach them.

How to Send a Thank You Letter or a Birthday Card to a Relative

Even though we live in an Internet world, and even elderly people these days enjoy Internet access, there are still times, such as when grandma is sick in the hospital, that mailing off an old-fashioned get-well card will be more appropriate than shooting off a text message or an e-mail. Be sure your student knows how to address an envelope, including adding a return address, and how much a first class stamp costs. If you have relatives in foreign countries, they also need to be aware that a first class stamp that does not indicate the postage amount is not valid.

How to Clean Leather Shoes

Eventually, your high school student, whose idea of dressing up until now has been to wear the kind of T-shirt that has a collar (polo shirt), or a skirt with a T-shirt and flip-flops, may find themselves in a job with a dress code. Some cinemas and restaurants require black pants and dress shoes. One of my sons was required to wear a tuxedo shirt and bow tie with black dress shoes and black dress pants to work in a cinema complex. A friend's son had a job in a pizza restaurant that had a dress code. His black leather shoes were constantly covered in grease and spilled drinks. While we rarely require our children to clean their tennis shoes, dress shoes sometimes need a polish. If your student intends to enter ROTC, they will certainly need this skill.

How to Separate the Lights from the Darks

Your student will be doing his or her own laundry (hopefully) from now on. On the first day at the campus laundry, will they know how to begin? Will they understand that they should also bring the bed sheets and the towels with them in their laundry bag? If they need special clothes for band or orchestra, do they know how to take care of the clothes? Investing in a few dry cleaning sheets that work in the dryer are a great way to help tide them over the dry cleaning until they get home.

How to Use Public Transportation

Many colleges do not allow freshmen to bring cars on campus for the first semester. Some students elect by themselves not to bring a car for the first year just to alleviate the number of things they have to worry about. Has your son or daughter ever taken the bus or the subway? Or have they ever ridden in a taxi? Will they know how much to tip the taxi driver? Or will they know to read a bus schedule or a subway map?

How Much to Tip

Is your student experienced at going by themselves to the hairdresser or taking care of a restaurant bill? Do they know how to calculate a tip and when it is appropriate to leave one? Even if you popped for the full meal plan, there will be times when your student ventures off-campus with a group of friends to a restaurant.

How to Spot Phishing or E-mail Scams

Your newly adult student, complete with his or her own credit card, ATM card, bank account, and laptop, is about to be unleashed without adult supervision onto the Internet Superhighway. Are you confident that they will be able to spot a phishing e-mail? Do you trust that they will recognize a scam if they are being asked for credit card information or their social security number over the Internet?

The basic rule of thumb is not to open any attachments if you do not recognize the source, do not click on e-mails that look like they are mass mailings from unknown sources, and never follow a Web site link from inside an e-mail unless you absolutely trust the sender. Always close the browser, re-open the browser, and type in the address from scratch in the URL box. This way your student will hit the bank's Web site, rather than the scammer's mocked up site. After visiting the bank or credit card Web site, always logoff and close the browser completely as a security measure against hackers finding an open connection to your bank account information. Re-launch the browser if you are going to continue surfing after doing financial business on the Internet.

Where to Buy Necessities

If your student is not experienced at doing his own shopping, it can be confusing for him to find the things he needs. Stu went without soap for two weeks when his boxes went missing. He claims he looked for it in the supermarket but did not know which aisle they kept it in. Will your student know what to do when he needs something not sold in the student bookstore?

Most students are familiar with doing an Internet search to locate things, but familiar applications, like MapQuest, generally provide driving instructions using freeways and fastest routes rather than giving directions for walking on foot or taking the bus. So, these tools can be confusing for a new student on how to find places off-campus, even when they know the address. A regular street map is a good idea and something you can easily acquire and leave with your student if you drop them off at the start of the semester.

How to Tell Analog Time

Your first thought might be "of course they can." Some of us were born before the proliferation of digital liquid crystal displays, and learning to tell time was a basic skill every one of us learned in school. But, strange as it seems to those of us who can remember the invention of the personal computer, children today grow up sometimes without ever learning to read the big hand and the little hand. This can lead to embarrassment.

How to Lace Their Shoes (not just tie them, but insert the laces from scratch)

Your son or daughter leaves the coddled environment of home where they were either driven everywhere by you or drove themselves to school, to soccer, to band, or whatever. Now they find they are a on a large campus which they have to cross on foot several times a day and their feet are covered with blisters because the shoes they wore when they were going everywhere by car just do not hold up when they are walking constantly. So they go and buy themselves a new pair of shoes. When they get home and open up the box, there are the shoes, and there, not in the shoes, are the laces. Can your student get the laces into the shoes without a meltdown?

How to Run the Virus Scan and Clean Up Viruses and Cookies

Are you or your spouse the ones that take care of the computer at home? Did you install a virus checker, and configure it to run scans automatically? Has the virus checker ever discovered a virus and asked you what it should do? Does it periodically ask you if you would like to purge the cookies? While we joke that our children know more about computers than we do, often we have sheltered them from the important stuff. Just because your son or daughter knows exactly how to find and download free iTunes, do not automatically assume they know how to protect their computer, which is about to be installed on a college campus network where budding hackers with the best brains in the country are being taught the very best and latest computer techniques and technologies.

If your student has to install the campus intranet virus checker, it may be necessary to uninstall the factory-installed application that came with the computer before it can run the new one properly.

E-mail Etiquette when Addressing a Professor or Person in Authority

Does your student instant message and text message

using abbreviations with no regard for capitalization and grammar? At some point in her college career, she will probably apply for a research position, make an appointment to see a professor, or otherwise communicate with people who have a long list of academic credentials, and often more than one Ph.D. If she addresses a professor in the same manner she address peers, she probably will not get much of a response.

It is never wrong to be a little formal. Even young, hip members of the professional staff will appreciate courtesy and respect. It is often wrong to be too casual. Teach your student how to address the professor by name, Dr. So-and-So or Mr. So-and-So, as appropriate, and end the e-mail with a polite sign off such as "regards," and then their full name.

How to Travel by Plane

Maybe your student is not going far from home and will not have to fly to college. However, even if this is the case, your chances of flying with them, whether on vacation or to college, are becoming fewer from this point forward. That means their chances of learning the ropes from you are also diminishing. Many of our children are seasoned travelers by the time they get to be 18, but there are plenty of people who have never traveled on a plane. Things to teach them include what they can carry on board, what they should pack into cargo, how to read departure and arrival boards, how to change terminals, and who to ask if they need help. Airports can be large, lonely places and sometimes just knowing who to ask a question can be confusing.

What to Do if their Laptop Stops Working or is Stolen

Computers are a student's lifeline. Most colleges are moving toward doing all business with the students online. The Internet, or college intranet, is vital for a student's survival. This is how they schedule classes, check grades, find out if bills are due, do their homework, and stay in touch with friends from home. Even though many colleges offer alternative access to computers, it often means a walk across campus on a cold, dark night. Your student enjoys their own personal access in their dorm room on their own schedule.

Many people these days purchase extended warranties for computers, some of them come with a one-year manufacturer's warranty, and some come with a three-month warranty. If your student's laptop breaks down, do they have a back-up plan? Do they know how to find out whether the campus has any kind of loaner program? Do they have a roommate who is willing to share in an emergency? Will they know what to do to get the computer fixed?

What if it simply "disappears?" Do they know whom to report it to, how to borrow one, buy another one, or otherwise find a way to be connected to the World Wide Web?

Some campuses have arrangements with certain

computer manufacturers and offer service bargains for those brands. If this is not the case, you can also check with the big-name electronic stores that offer computer service to find the one closest to the campus. If you have purchased a three-year warranty, see what the return policy is. If the student has to bundle up the computer, mail it off, and wait six weeks, it may be a better option to do without the warranty and just take it down to the nearest authorized repair shop.

What to Do if Their Car Breaks Down Halfway Home

Your student has one last lab class on the Tuesday before Thanksgiving that runs until 8 p.m., and then he is free. You are expecting him to leave early Wednesday morning and expect to see him sometime Wednesday afternoon. But, your freshman student misses you more than you think. On a whim, he decides that if he hops in the car directly after lab and rides through the night, he can be home sometime in the wee hours and sneak into the house ready to surprise you when you wake up in the morning. Everything is going according to plan until his car grinds inexplicably to a halt on a black, lonely part of the highway, 50 miles from the closest gas station. What now?

If your student drives to college, equipping him with an automobile membership, such as AAA, and an in-car cell phone charger are good options. Depending on the level of service you choose, you get free towing to the nearest repair shop, free gas delivery, and free diagnostic checks.

A credit card for an emergency stay at a motel is also a good safety device.

What to Do if They Get in a Car Wreck

Unfortunately, some of our children have already had their first car accident before they go to college. But in many cases, the first thing they probably did was call you. What about when you are not there? Will they have the presence of mind not to be bullied into admitting liability when they know they were not at fault? Will they have the courage to insist on calling the police when the other party rear-ended them and is trying to talk them into walking away with a dented fender or broken taillight?

CHAPTER 6

Packing for College

There are some predictable things you know your student will need and some things you may not know in advance. The biggest thing to remember is that student dorms are small. Girls tend to pack more than boys do, and overall they tend to do more decorating and rearranging than boys. Girls also tend to be cleaner and more organized in general. Most colleges require freshmen to live on campus, and most colleges require them to have a roommate.

This means you can sometimes check in with your roommate before you travel to negotiate who brings the microwave, the coffee pot, and other equipment. There are also certain regulations to check on that will vary from college to college and from dorm to dorm. Some regulations restrict the use of microwaves above a certain power level and prohibit the use of things like electric grills, while others encourage the use of these. Some dorms will let you rearrange the room any way you like, while others do not.

The best plan is not to buy anything in the way of electronics or furnishings until you know for sure which dorm or living complex your student has been assigned.

Once you know that, you can figure out what comes standard (some come with refrigerators and microwaves and many do not) and what is allowed or prohibited.

If the first time you are seeing the room is the day your student moves in, you may want to allow extra time on the day of arrival to shop for furnishings, such as chairs and rugs, rather than buying them in advance only to find out there is nowhere to put them. Older colleges can have shockingly tiny spaces.

The Georgia Tech Parents Handbook recommends making a list and then cutting it in half, using a storage unit over the summer, and pre-ordering items in the destination town and having them put on hold at the store for you to pick up when you arrive.

It is also a good idea to bring or buy something that locks so the computer and other valuables can be safely stored when your student is not in the room. She may be perfectly responsible herself and careful to lock her own room, but her roommate may not. Most theft that occurs on campus is because students leave their rooms unlocked and unattended.

Clothing

The student uniform is jeans and a T-shirt, accessorized with well-worn athletic shoes and little else. In winter it does not change much, but it may be augmented with a sweatshirt, a hoodie, or occasionally, a jacket of some kind. In warmer climes, the jeans may be replaced by shorts. Bearing in mind that the average student only does laundry when their clean clothes run out, if you have additional money to spare and wish to spend it on your child's clothing, you should consider purchasing as many of these as possible so that your student can concentrate on the finer things in life, like frat parties and studying. However, do not waste money on more formal clothes. Exceptions to this may be if your son or daughter participates in band or orchestra, requires athletic clothing for sports, or will be participating in interviews for internships.

Underwear is relatively cheap and easy to pack and, generally, one can never have too many pairs of undies or socks.

I packed one dress shirt for each of my sons and one dress pair of pants and dress shoes. I am quite sure they never get worn, but I could not send them off on their own in clean conscience without at least one decent outfit, just in case. After freshman year I rarely bothered with their wardrobe, leaving it entirely up to them. They know what they wear.

Bringing a Car to Campus

Some colleges have rules about freshmen bringing cars to campus. Some will allow freshmen to have cars the second semester of freshman year, while others will not allow a car on campus for the entire freshman year. Still others have no policy and allow freshmen to bring cars on campus immediately.

Maintaining a car, especially an older car, requires both

planning and dealing with the unexpected. You have to put gas in it, pay for a parking permit, keep it running in the winter, deal with breakdowns, and potentially, accidents. If campus is far from home, breaking down between college and home may not be inevitable, but it has a high likelihood of occurring at eventually unless your student can afford a very nice car.

If it is going to breakdown on the way home, you can bet that it will happen:

- Over Thanksgiving, because this is the shortest holiday that your student will probably come home for, and has the least amount of time to spare on glitches

- Along the loneliest stretch of highway where cell phone coverage is patchy at best and the distance to the nearest service garage is 50 miles

Ironically, after I wrote these words, this exact thing happened to my son. His car broke down on the way home for Thanksgiving on a stretch of highway with patchy cell phone coverage.

If your campus has rules about bringing a car, naturally you should be guided by those. But if the college allows freshmen to bring cars to campus, and you and your student make the decision to bring a car, then at the very least you should ensure your student has a strategy for coping with car trouble. A friend's son decided to drive home through the night. When his car broke down he was forced to stay in a motel for a couple of days while spare parts were ordered and installed in his car.

Most campuses have good transportation alternatives for students, including reduced-cost bus service and a bicycle-friendly environment.

Some students will go through anything to have a car. If students are car smart, know how to cope with car trouble, and are financially able to run a car, there is no reason why they should not have their car with them. However, if you sense that a new environment, college level math, and coping with their own independence will be quite enough for starters, you may try to dissuade them from adding car maintenance to the list of things they will have to learn to deal with by themselves.

Ian took his bike the first year, and his car the second year. His dad or I made the drive back and forth to Nebraska the first couple of times and then he got in the habit of taking the Greyhound bus (which incidentally is cheaper than paying the gas for driving yourself). Georgia Tech does not allow freshmen to have cars on campus their first semester, and it is far enough away that it did not make any sense to send Stu in his car. So he travels back and forth by plane.

The scariest thing in my mind about not having a car is that they are likely to ride with other students. The idea of a bunch of male students driving around together late at night, and potentially after drinking alcohol, makes me very nervous. I remind myself that more students graduate than not, and I have given them both as good a foundation as I possibly can with respect to drinking and driving and peer pressure. The rest is up to them.

Sheets, Towels, Dishes, and Other Miscellaneous Items

Dorm room beds typically use the extended-length twin size sheets (known as twin XL). From the moment your student accepts an offer, you will be inundated with exclusive offers for cheap polyester twin XL sheets that the advertiser will assure you "are guaranteed to fit." There is nothing wrong with accepting these offers, and it can be quite convenient to shop through the mail. However, be aware that almost every department store carries these sheets nowadays, and you can find good bargains in the summer white sales.

Whatever you buy, your student has to:

- Carry back and forth between school and home

- Store in their dorm room

- Launder from time to time

I do not recommend more than two towels and one set of sheets. Girls may use more towels, but boys most definitely only use one. The less they have to cart to the laundry the better.

Even if you have purchased the three-meals-a-day

plan, there will be days when students do not eat in the dining hall for whatever reason and feel like staying in their room. It is a good idea to send them off with an easy-to-care-for plastic plate and bowl, a favorite mug and a knife, fork, and spoon. I packed a dishcloth and sponge also, and noticed that these came back in their original plastic wrapping after one year at school.

The best rule is stick to essentials and do not buy anything superfluous.

Stu asked me for an umbrella and claims it comes in handy when it rains and he wants to walk across campus.

Ian took a heavy coat to Nebraska his first year and left it at home his second year, stating that he preferred his lighter fleece jacket, even in the bitter cold of a Midwestern winter.

Food

Students will buy what they fancy when they need it, but it is a good idea to stock them up with some bottles of water, soda, and other drinks they enjoy, along with a few cans of soup, ramen, and other microwaveable goodies. Keeping a supply of drinks is probably the hardest thing when you are on a dining hall plan. It means that every time you are thirsty you have to pay vending machine prices or buy individual bottles or cans at the bookstore or campus convenience store, ripping through meager college funds at an alarming rate. Buying economical fridge packs of soda means they have to carry them, often on foot, for a mile or more from the store. Thoughtful parents will leave their children stocked with drinks before they leave them on campus on the first day.

School Supplies

Of all the supplies that students need in their first year away from home, these are the easiest to come by on a college campus. Just about every college campus has a bookstore sells school supplies, but some things will not be as cheap as you think they should be in a store that caters to college students on low incomes.

If you are economy-minded, it is a good idea to pick up some basics, such as paper and pens, and maybe some folders or binders, at a discount superstore such as Target or Wal-Mart. The prices will be better. However, if you forget something, or if your student finds out in the early days of class that special supplies will be needed, it is not usually difficult to find such things in the college bookstore.

If you have been used to buying "back-to-school" supplies for your student, and now you are encouraging them to buy their own supplies, you will be amazed at how few things they actually need. In addition, they will use even less than they purchase.

A stapler, a pair of scissors, a stick of glue, and a three-hole punch will probably come in handy. If your student is doing math, the professor will probably recommend a specific calculator so it is not worth getting one in advance. Take whatever calculator your student used in high school with you just in case, and wait for the professor's recommendation before buying a new one.

Computers, Laptops, and Other Electronics

Before you rush out and buy your student a new laptop for college, check on requirements with the university or college in advance. Some colleges do not require computers or laptops, while others not only require them, but also have specific required specifications, including minimum amount of memory, screen size, and software. Some colleges specify whether a laptop or a desktop is required, and some provide loaner services on campus for students who, for whatever reason, do not own a computer and are unable to purchase one.

If your student takes a computer to college, be sure to invest a few dollars in a surge protector so that bad weather or high voltage surges do not ruin the computer.

Also, check before you buy a printer. Some colleges offer students printing services free of charge, while others do not. Some students come to arrangements with their roommates, and others like to be completely independent. The well-equipped student these days sets up their own mini-suite of office equipment in their dorm room. This can be a little overwhelming to some parents who still think of computers as somewhat of a luxury item rather than a necessity.

Many dorm rooms accommodate high-speed Internet

and cable television, so many students bring their own T.V. Laptops sometimes come with T.V. tuners, so one piece of equipment can serve two purposes. T.V. shows can also be accessed on the Internet, so the lack of a television need not be a problem if your student has a laptop and an Internet connection in the dorm room.

Make sure your student pays attention to anti-virus software. Some campuses provide this free of charge and require security tools to be installed prior to using the campus intranet. Others do not make recommendations. You can find out in advance what is required for the campus your student is planning to attend. If none is provided, you should make sure the laptop or desktop is adequately protected by ensuring a current version of anti-virus or security suite software is installed and configured to update itself automatically and to run at least once a week on your student's computer.

If you need help, find out about anti-virus software at a local computer store. I installed and configured a security suite on my computer-savvy son's laptop and taught him how to use it. Even so, by Thanksgiving his laptop was so choked with viruses off the Internet that the anti-virus software itself could not even run. As it turns out the computer spent three weeks in the campus computer service department during final exams and when it came home at Christmas, still not working right, we ended up having to reinstall the operating system.

CHAPTER 7

Departure Day

In the weeks preceding the departure day, you have probably spent a lot of time thinking through the best day to go, the best time to arrive, how to travel, what to bring, and so on. As you plan the departure, there are a couple of things to consider about the arrival.

Logistics

One thing you need to think about is what day to arrive. Campuses usually open to freshmen a little ahead of other students. There are advantages and disadvantages to arriving early. It gives your student plenty of time to settle in, get their room arranged, and even get first pick of the beds if they arrive ahead of their roommate. There is a buzz of excitement the first weekend prior to classes. Fraternities may be having extravagant street parties to get students interested in them. On some campuses, the pungent aroma of barbecue pig, bratwurst, seafood, and other tasty treats fill the air. There is plenty to eat offered in the street. There is a hustle and bustle of parents and students coming and going, bearing groceries and furnishings, and struggling under the weight of boxes of water and soda as they load up dorm rooms with all the comforts of home. The stairwells and elevators in the residence halls are congested with this family trying to bring up a refrigerator and that family trying to lug a chest of drawers up to the third floor.

An article in the *Georgia Tech Parents Handbook* recommends that on move-in day you pack some patience and wear comfortable shoes. They go on to recommend investing in a dolly. You will want to find out in advance if the residence hall has an elevator — some do not. If your student has a room on the third or fourth level, you could be in for some heavy exercise. Further, they point out the differences between moving in a girl as opposed to a boy:

> *"If you're moving boys in, it takes the back seat and trunk of the car. If you're moving girls in, it takes a minivan with all the seats removed, a small truck, and three trips to Target and/or Office Depot."*

Whether you are moving a boy or a girl, most parents who have done this before recommend not packing too many things, unless you have visited the campus and know the room size is above average. Dorm rooms can be very small, and it can be hard to find a place for everything, even if you were able to fit it all in your car. Advice we hear over and over again from seasoned college parents is to plan on buying some things after you arrive.

Arriving early gives you time to walk around campus with your student and find classrooms, the post office, the bookstore, the library, the student union, and other places of interest.

Some residence halls offer special icebreaker events for freshmen and dorm residents.

On the other hand, in the days preceding class, if you do not know anyone yet and have an introverted personality, arriving too early can lead to loneliness and emptiness. After parents leave and there are still two or three days before classes start, it can seem as though everyone has something to do and somewhere to go except you.

You may decide to make a family vacation out of it by leaving early and spending a few days in the new college town. However, remember that you may want to plan things so that your student can have some time alone. If they end up making friends on the first day, and there are some activities going on they would like to go do with their new friend, you must be prepared to give your student some space. Plan on doing some sightseeing in town by yourself or with the rest of the family, and touch base with your student from time to time over the days you are there. Do not plan on spending all of your time with your student. Having you there in the background can be a great comfort in case anything goes wrong in the first couple of days, but do not let it become a burden to your student.

I recommend not planning to arrive the moment the

doors open (it is never good to be the first one arriving at a party) unless you really do think you need several days to move in. It is best to plan to arrive the early part of the weekend before the first day of class. Perhaps plan to arrive Friday night or Saturday morning, depending on how far you have to travel. That way you will arrive in the midst of the bustle and not at the last minute. It is fun to arrive when there is already plenty of life on campus, and you do not want to miss the fun stuff that often does not begin until Friday or Saturday night.

Remember to check the practical things as well, like where to go to pick up the room key and what times the dorm office is open.

Deciding Whether to Stay and Unpack

You want to make sure your student is settled in before you leave and all the underwear is neatly folded in the drawer, the computer is installed and online, and the pens and notebooks are in easy reach on the desk. But should you help your student unpack?

I say no. Even though there is plenty going on the weekend before class starts, your student will still be spending quite a bit of time alone those first few days. Unpacking is the one thing your student has to do after you leave. It can fill a void and give them something constructive to do. Do not take that away.

The exception to that is taking care of any difficult problems. Getting the computer installed and on the campus network can be daunting for some students. It may require purchasing a special cable or installing the campus anti-virus software. Storing a musical instrument or any other special piece of equipment not being kept in the room is another thing that you can help with. Those things are hard. But as for arranging the room and putting clothes away, those are things that students should do for themselves. It helps to give them a sense of belonging. Do not worry that they fold their jeans instead of hanging them or that they put their underwear in the drawer with the books instead of in the drawer with the socks. This is their room now, and they need to arrange it to suit themselves.

Shopping for Supplies

While it may not be the best idea to help your student unpack their belongings, if there is one thing a parent on campus is good for, it is picking up the tab for last-minute supplies. Even if your student has a meal plan, they will appreciate a stock of soda, bottled water, or sports drinks. Another handy thing to leave behind with your student is a day planner or calendar so he can keep track of when assignments are due and monitor how close the holidays are.

Meeting the Roommate

I do not believe it is important for parents to meet the roommate, but most of us are curious, and it makes us feel better to have at least some kind of picture in our heads of who are child is living with by the time we say goodbye. Ian was paired with a sophomore who transferred in from another school. I thought it was rather curious that they would pair a freshman with a sophomore, but they were both new to the University of Lincoln, Nebraska, and it seemed to work out all right even though they did not become best friends.

A friend's son was paired with someone he absolutely could not get along with, and he spent several weeks being transferred to a different room. He then transferred out of that college altogether and moved to another college for sophomore year.

Stu hit it off with his roommate right away. I took them both out to dinner the first night we arrived and I had the opportunity to observe them getting along. Stu tells me that he, his roommate, and some other friends on the same floor are looking for accommodations together for next year.

Whether or not your child is destined to become life-long friends with his or her roommate or whether it will turn into a saga, it is up to your student to make do, to seek a change, or to spend time looking for their roommate's "good" side to make it through the rest of the year. You cannot change it and you cannot fix it. You can only be there for moral support and listen with feeling if your student needs to talk about it.

Saying Goodbye

The day of departure can often be so busy that you barely have time to stop and think. Until that dreaded moment when everything is in place, it is time to leave, and you and your student are standing face to face with nothing more to do than say goodbye to each other.

In the book *I'll Miss You Too* by Margo Woodacre and her daughter, Steffany Bane, Steff describes saying goodbye to her mother:

> *"It was difficult saying goodbye to them [her parents] and I tried not to appear upset — just a thank you and a quick unemotional hug. I was worried about Mom crying because I knew that would start me crying."*

A parent writing about her experience in the *Georgia Tech Handbook* advises parents to prepare themselves for tears from yourself and your child.

> *"I was surprised when Rachel choked up first. It was awkward making the final break, knowing when to actually leave. I waited until she said I could go."*

However much you would like to cling to your child and hold them to you forever, do not make it a long drawn out goodbye. That only makes it harder for them to say goodbye.

When Ian left, his dad drove him to campus and all I had to do was stand in the driveway and wave as he left to go to his dad's house. Even so, I found myself thinking about him all weekend long. I wondered, "Where is he now?" I wondered if he had seen his room; I wondered what he thinks about his roommate; and I wondered if he was lonely and scared on the first night.

I will never forget the hollow feeling in the pit of my stomach as I gave Stu, my other son, a quick hug and turned to go, knowing that I was leaving him with only a few things that I had scrambled to buy for him at the last minute. He was thousands of miles from home and I had no easy way to help him from here on out. Stu had signed up for a cooperative program. At the end of the first year he would start to alternate one semester of work and one semester of school. The summer of his first year would most likely be spent working as an intern. Saying goodbye was especially hard because I knew he may not have summers free, as Ian did, to come home and be with the family. I had probably spent my last full summer with Stu.

And yet, even as I walked away, he was already getting along with his roommate and the two of them were heading off that evening to explore campus and attend some street parties courtesy of the fraternity houses.

SECTION

2

The Student's Experience

CHAPTER 8

Alone at Last

A girl who used the Internet name "Xtina" posted the following on "Yahoo! Answers":

> *"Was anyone else miserable their first few weeks of college? Or is it just me? I feel like I'm living in this place where I don't know anybody. I mean, I meet people in class, but the classes are so big you never really sit next to them again so it's hard to get to know them. I don't really have anything in common with my roommates. I don't do anything other than go to class, come back, watch T.V., and do homework, go to bed and wake up and do it all over again. It's so terrible because my old life wasn't like that at all. I want to get involved and do fun things at school but it's hard when you don't even have one other person to go check them out with or even one other person to go to fun events with. I wanted to rush for a sorority but it's going to be weird if I go by myself. I*

*don't know...basically what I'm asking
is if anyone else felt this way and if so
did it get better?"*

Xtina's posting tugged at my heart. The answer to her question is that many new college freshmen feel the same way, and for the vast majority it does get better, but not in the first few weeks, sometimes not even in the first semester. Xtina's emotional posting sums up the college experience for most entering freshmen.

The answers she received in response to her posting corroborated her experience. Some reported that they felt the same way. Older students recommended that she get out and join a club or sorority to start making friends. A college senior commented on Xtina's remark that she never sat next to the same student twice. This student told Xtina the person sitting next to her in the big lecture hall was feeling just as lonely and lost.

For most college students, moving into a dorm is the first experience moving out of the family home. For most, it is the first extended period away from home. For students who have participated in summer camps, international trips, and other adventures, there may be an unspoken anticipation that they are about to embark on the same sort of adventure. After all, the college years are supposed to be the best years of our lives. These unwitting students trundle off to college expecting life to be one long party. And for some, it can become so. But even for extrovert party animals, the first few weeks can be overwhelmingly lonely.

College is a different experience than being away from your family for a two or three week stay at summer camp. First of all, students are completely on their own. There is no umbrella organization to take care of them and no volunteer parent escorts to turn to or feel safe with. When you attend summer camp, you tend to go with friends, and you are among people you know. In college, that is not the case for most students.

The first weekend, when you arrive with your parents, endorses the expectation of a summer camp experience. The atmosphere when you arrive during move-in weekend is lively, entertaining, and full excitement. However, reality quickly sets in.

The First Night Alone

Move-in day is long and hectic. Your student was most likely up much earlier than usual to make last minute preparations and undertake the journey. It may have been a long car or plane ride. You may have spent more than one day on the journey. Students probably spend most of that time in nervous anticipation wondering what their room would be like and whether they would like their roommate. They may have wondered if they will figure out the way back to their room when they venture out on campus or if they will be able to find the bookstore, the lecture halls, and the library by themselves.

When you both finally arrive, a whirlwind of activity keeps you busy; getting boxes from the car, finding a store for last minute supplies, getting the computer wired up, and wandering around campus becoming oriented. As the parent, you try and cram in every last thing you can think of to prepare your student for campus life alone, and finding classrooms, lecture halls, the pharmacy, and the late-night convenience store. Maybe you use the last few hours treating your student to one last family dinner in a nice restaurant.

Then You Depart

Ian's Dad took him to college. They stopped off along the way to visit with Grandma and Grandpa, spending two days en route. Dan dropped Ian at his residence hall, helped him unpack his belongings, and took time to tour the campus. He set up Ian's computer and helped him install the anti-virus software and a discounted copy of Microsoft Word that he purchased at the bookstore.

I asked Ian what it felt like when his dad left to go home after the two days they had spent traveling together.

> *"I felt kind of abandoned, like everyone was going back to their normal lives without me and I was stuck having to adjust to something completely new. I think I felt more sad than scared."*

Your student looks wistfully around at the last unpacked box and checks the time. It is still early in the evening, and your freshman silently calculates that it will take 10 minutes to unpack it. Then they are faced with the prospect of a long, lonely evening stretching ahead.

The room is tiny and you only get half of it. The bed is hard and looks very different from the one they are used to at home. Even with their own bedding (which may be new and unfamiliar), it does not look like it is really theirs yet. It may be a loft bed, and they may have to climb up before they can even sit on the edge of it. There is no sofa to lounge on and watch T.V. from, except down the hall. But the hall looks long, uninviting and populated with strangers who all look, to your unprepared student, like they know what they are doing and where they are going.

Students may or may not have their own T.V. in the room. This may be the first time in their life that they have had to think up some way to spend their free time without watching T.V. If they want to watch the one down the hall, that means leaving the room, venturing out, and then perhaps finding it tuned to a channel they are not interested in. Not only that but they are terrified to leave their room in the beginning for fear of forgetting their key.

Even if there is a fridge in the room, there are none of their favorite things in it to pick on — just soda, maybe, and water. No leftover Chinese food from the night before or deli meat to make sandwiches from — none of their favorite cheese or peanut butter. The absence of food close to hand can be intimidating.

Ian told me he worried about food the most on the first night.

"I was most nervous about being hungry all the time. I didn't know how good the dining halls were going to be, and I was used to being able to eat whenever I wanted to at home."

It even seems daunting to go the bathroom. There is a dire lack of privacy in residence hall bathrooms. Stu told me that the first few days in Smith residence hall everyone was reluctant to take a shower. They found themselves showering at odd times to try and find a moment when no-one else was using the bathroom.

Right after you leave your student, they may pull out their cell phone and look at your number 10 times that night without hitting send. Some of them do call you, or you call them, and perhaps they convince you they are doing fine. Girls are more likely to admit they are lonely than boys, but most boys feel just as lonely as girls at this stage of the game.

If your student has met his roommate the chances are the two of them will spend the evening together looking for something to do around campus. There will be plenty of activities to choose from as the first week of the semester gets underway. However, students arrive on campus with friends, which is not often the case, they are going to be feeling shy, awkward and out of their element the first night, even after they have chosen to spend it in the company of a roommate and possibly other students from the residence hall. Despite the rush of activities on campus, some students, especially those with a tendency to be more introverted, may choose to stay alone in their room and gather their composure after the hurly-burly of arrival day.

Despite the holiday camp atmosphere of the first couple of days, students know somewhere in the back of their minds that in a day or two they will be sitting in class. They know they will be learning new and important information. They understand there is a need to make new friends. But on this first, lonely night they have not quite connected with it all.

Even the most confident and outgoing of students is likely to feel a little drained or overwhelmed by this point. Deep down they are tired. There have been a lot of new experiences, sights, sounds and smells to take in. Their senses have been overloaded and they have been emotionally stretched. They are running on adrenaline by this point. It is all a bit surreal and dreamy.

The Early Weeks

After classes start, the first couple of weeks seem to go by in a haze of new experiences that are difficult to process and absorb immediately. It usually takes a few weeks before it all slows down and students come to the realization that this is real, it is dragging on, there are classes to attend, and there is no escape. This is neither home nor summer camp. It is college. And despite all the fun activities and new friends, assignments are due and the dining hall is serving the exact same menu again this week as it has every week since school began.

After the first couple of weeks, the organized social

activities fade as the semester gets in full swing and it is harder to find things to do. Even though they know some names and faces, and they know the way to all their classes, it has not been long enough to form strong friendships. They miss the close, familiar friends they had in high school and miss coming home each night to their own room, their own home, their own sofa or favorite chair, and, yes, they even miss seeing you.

Perhaps the hardest part of moving away from home is building a new framework for how to spend your time. Classes are often at odd times of day, some are early in the day, and some are later in the evening. Some days you have several classes and other days you have one or two, or perhaps none at all. The rhythm of each day is uneven and unstructured. You have to plan your meals around the time the dining halls are open. You have a lot of free time and do not know what to do with it — then, all of a sudden, a homework assignment is due and you run out of time to work on it.

On the Yahoo! Answers site, Xtina had an outpouring of responses from fellow freshmen assuring her that she was not alone. Responses included advice from older students as well as other freshmen, and she heard from both male and female students. More than one response advised her to get involved in clubs and activities. As it turned out, Xtina joined a sorority, made great friends, and was having a much better time later in the semester.

My son Ian has always been an independent child, both socially and emotionally. He was quite used to making his own meals and entertaining himself with video games and his computer, and even though he has two brothers, he seldom seemed to need them. He had been away from home by himself at least once before he went to college. I was worried that he may find college challenging academically, but I did not think he would have much trouble adapting to life on his own because of his independent nature. I knew that most students experience some degree of homesickness in the first few weeks, reaching a peak for many around about the twelfth week or so. At freshman orientation, I learned what to expect and waited for symptoms to appear, standing ready to offer support when called on. But I was not aware of Ian going through it.

He called every week, and always painted a picture that everything was going fine. He talked about the classes he was taking, how the football team was doing, and what clubs he was going to. He never talked about being homesick. Once I got a short e-mail from him hinting that he was missing home, and I wrote back to comfort him, telling him that homesickness is normal and most students go through it in one form or another during their first year. He replied, telling me that he was not homesick and everything was fine.

I thought maybe we had escaped the terrible time that they warned us about in freshman orientation, and perhaps Ian handled things better than some students.

But after freshman year was over, sometime during summer vacation, the truth came out. Ian talked about feeling sick and throwing up the first few days of the semester. Far from gaining the "freshman fifteen," he reported losing weight during the first few weeks because he could not eat. He felt terribly lost and alone. Every college has a high proportion of local students. Ian watched local students go home on weekends, and he felt disadvantaged because he did not have his car. He was in a town he was unfamiliar with, and he did not know where to go off campus to get anything.

Colleges understand that students are vulnerable in these first few weeks. This is the time most college students drop out, and decide the experience is too much for them. Most colleges have many resources in place to help students deal with their new lives, but your student may not reach out to them.

It is a good idea to keep your guard up when you communicate with students during this time. Look for signs and be in touch. Do not call every night or overwhelm them with e-mails, but just be around. A quick e-mail or a phone message now and then goes a long way, even if they do not reply. This is also the best time to send care packages, handwritten letters or a quick note that says, "Thinking of you." Let them know you are available, but remember that they need time to sort this part out for themselves. Remind them Thanksgiving will be here before they know it.

When Stu went to Atlanta I booked him a one-way flight and bought myself a round trip ticket. Stu was shocked. He told me the reality of that moment, of getting a one way ticket to college, made the reality of leaving seem much bigger and more real than it had before. He said it made going to college seem scary. I decided to book his ticket home for Thanksgiving before I left him at college and gave him the e-ticket to store in a folder. I told him when he was lonely to look at it and remember that he would be home soon. He told me later that just knowing he had a ticket home made the loneliness more tolerable in the early weeks.

CHAPTER 9

Settling In

Once the first couple of weeks are over and classes are underway, students begin to prepare for their first college exams — midterms. At this point, enhanced by the stresses of the academic side of college and often lower grades than expected, loneliness and homesickness can reach a peak. It is important to establish some support tools early on. *The Georgia Tech Parents Program Handbook* recommends getting involved.

> *"...join something, anything — to which the student can belong and build a support group. It really helps for them to have someone looking out for them and helping them along."*

Having a place to go every week, on the same night, helps to create structure for your student. Seeing people on a regular basis who share the same interests can be an anchor in a stormy sea. When you see the same faces over and over again, they become familiar and comfortable. There are a multitude of different organizations available on a college campus. Encourage your student to try two or three different ones until they finds something they can relate strongly to.

It is wise to join more than one because sometimes the meetings dwindle, the club suffers from lack of support and stops meeting. So it is good to have a fall-back position; something else you belong to. On the other hand, if you sign up for too many it becomes a hectic juggling act — deciding where you need to be, which one to choose when activities overlap, or simply forgetting to show up. Sign up for two to four to begin, with the aim of whittling it down to just one or two over the course of the semester. Then try to develop the habit of attending regularly because this helps set a routine. Routine and structure also reinforce a sense of well-being, of belonging, and of having one's life in order.

Fraternities and Sororities

Is it a good thing or a bad thing to join a sorority or a fraternity? Will your child be in danger if they are subjected to "hazing," a rite of passage required of rushees to become members of a fraternity or sorority? Myths, as well as cold hard facts, and horror stories abound about hazing.

These are not easy questions to answer. Every student (supported by parents) should do thorough research before pledging a fraternity or sorority because they can be different from each other. Various requirements for joining cover a wide range from the sedate to the ridiculous. Hazing still goes on, although not to equal degrees, despite being banned by most colleges. Pledging can take many different forms within Greek houses on the same campus, as well as from college to college.

There are positive aspects to being in a fraternity or sorority. In general, Greek students maintain higher than average grade point averages. They provide a sense of brotherhood or sisterhood and belonging at a time when students are in need of support. They can also provide an environment for academic mentoring. Often, Greek houses are equipped to foster a sound learning environment, and while their weekly parties may be the talk of the campus, there is a camaraderie in a fraternity that is unrivalled by joining any other type of club or organization on campus.

They often boast good facilities for computers access and quiet study. Of course, not all members get to live in the houses; it is possible to belong to a fraternity or sorority and still live in a regular dorm room in a residence hall.

When you are researching Greek chapters remember that there are chapters to cover just about any kind of interest. Not all of them are supported on every campus so you need to find out which ones are on campus and what each stands for. There are fraternities and sororities for almost every kind of interest. Some attract party types, some are focused around a specific religion, and some center around career aspirations or political persuasion.

Greek houses do a lot of recruiting and offer plenty of recruiting activities during pre-orientation visits, during freshman orientation, and during the first week of the fall semester. Encourage your student to explore several of them and understand their values and charters before pledging. Some campuses and Greek chapters offer deferred recruiting. This means that freshmen students are no longer accepted in the first semester, but Rush Week is deferred until the second semester. This allows freshmen a semester to explore the Greek chapter they think they are interested and get to know its members.

Of course, acceptance is usually subject to approval by the members of the fraternity or sorority and is not guaranteed.

Time Management

Time management can be a make it or break it deal for a lot of students. In the words used in the *Georgia Tech Parents Handbook*, *"It's often the difference between success and failure."*

There is little structure for an undisciplined student. Some lectures can have upward of 100 students, some have as many as 250. If you do not show up for class, no one notices. As Xtina reported in her Yahoo! posting, you may never sit next to the same person twice.

Likewise, if you do not turn in your assignments on time, there is no one breathing down your neck or calling your parents to remind you that you are behind with your work. A student may suddenly realize there is an essay due in a class the next day and may end up working through the night to get it turned in on time. This, in turn, results in poor concentration the next day in class. This sets in motion a downward spiral of stress and fatigue that may lead to lower grades, not just in the class with the essay but in all classes.

The first few weeks, with a hectic schedule of activities and social engagements, sets the stage for late nights and crazy work schedules that permeates the rest of the college experience. This is nothing like the life your student was used to in high school, where coming home at night was mandatory and mom or dad was always hovering in the background ensuring homework was done on time. Students who lack self-discipline in the time management department will have a rocky road to travel in college.

During freshman orientation at the University of Nebraska, senior students highly advocated the use of a day planner. I like the kind with big spaces for each day that opens to a whole month in one view. This is easier to use than the weekly kind because you have to flip through several pages to find out what is coming up in the next couple of weeks and it makes it harder to see if an assignment is due early in the following week. Some people like the kind that hangs on the wall and you can write on it with a dry-erase marker, again so you can plan the whole month at once.

Encourage your student to write not just when the assignment is due but what days and times they plan on putting in some work on it. They should also write down any club activities and other things they plan to do so they can keep their whole life straight just by looking in a single place. If they keep it open on their desk it is easier to get in the habit of looking at it every day and they do not run the risk of letting several days pass without remembering to open it.

At Colorado State University a senior student talked about how overwhelmed she was in freshman year. Clearly a high energy personality, she had joined four clubs on campus, was working part-time, and was carrying 16 class credits. She talked about how difficult it was juggling all those activities and knowing where she had to be when, until she invested in a day planner. Then she was able to lay it all out, and see what was happening. She realized she had completely overscheduled her life. She resolved her problem by dropping a couple of activities and reported becoming a much happier person, as well as more organized.

Do not just tell your student to buy a planner. Go out and buy it for them. A day planner is not exciting. Your student is saving their scant resources for the latest DVD or some other more exciting thing. A day planner is a tedious supply to have to buy, but they may use it if you buy it for them and leave it open on their desk when you drop them off.

The most important tool in helping students master time management is by setting the expectation early on, preferably a long time before they even get to college, that the objective of going in the first place is to graduate. Not only that, but to graduate with a decent GPA. While high school students are engaged in visiting and researching colleges, they are fed a steady diet of information about the fun side of college. We emphasize sports, joining organizations and clubs, and talk about parties and social activities. When they visit, colleges try to pump them up by offering them overnight stays in a fraternity house or a residence hall. Often, they pair them with older students who have settled into college life and can show them a good time. This raises freshmen expectations to thinking a whirling social life is required. Few students arrive at college having heard how hard it is to graduate, how they have to knuckle down and get through the hard parts, and how they will suffer terrible homesickness in their first few weeks. We do not always remember to tell them that they need perseverance, patience, and lots of trips to the library or to their academic advisor to do well.

It can come as a rude awakening when they get their first grades, or the results of their first mid-term. It pays to help temper their expectations from time to time before they leave home that their grade point average is their primary concern and studying must come first.

If they do not lose sight of the end goal, they will eventually come up with a routine that works for them. Do not worry if it is not the routine you would prefer them to follow, as long as they are working it out.

The Roommate

A lot of colleges do not offer freshmen the choice of a single room. They do this for a reason. College life can be lonely the first few weeks, and even if you get stuck with a roommate that you do not especially get along with, it can be better than being totally alone.

A child who has never shared a bedroom will possibly have a harder time than a child who grew up sharing a room with a sibling. However, I think it has more to do with personality matching.

Ian looked forward somewhat nervously to having a roommate. I worried because he needed a lot of alone time, but at the same time, I knew he would be slow to get out and meet people. He was paired with a sophomore who transferred in from another university — which was a bit of a surprise to me, but it seemed to work out well enough, although they were never best friends. The sophomore was outgoing and invited Ian to go along with him to various activities. Since he was a bit older, even though he was new to Nebraska, he found it easy to get around and was able to pass information along to Ian about how to do this and that and where to go for certain things.

Stu was paired with a student who lived locally in Georgia. Rahul was from an Indian background, which opened Stu's eyes to different cultural experiences. They became great friends, and shared music, books, and friends. Stu was invited to Rahul's house in Atlanta several times and enjoyed eating Indian food with his family and having a family tie in a lonely city.

A friend of ours, let us call him Kyle, also grew up never having to share a bedroom, and did not fare so well. He spent his freshman year in a big school in the Northwest. He knew right away he did not like his roommate but he tried to make it work. Despite his best efforts, Kyle found the roommate boorish and dirty. He used Kyle's things without permission and generally made life miserable. Several weeks into the semester Kyle put himself on a waiting list to change rooms. After several more weeks, he was able to make a switch to a different living arrangement where he had his own room and shared a kitchen and bathroom. In the end, following some other bad experiences, Kyle transferred out of that college and settled on a school in another part of the state where he finished his degree.

Most students start college with the intention of getting along with their assigned roommate. The vast majority either do get along or can live with the situation well enough to make it through the first year. But after the first few weeks have passed by and you are not getting along with your roommate, it can be stressful, and the stress can pour out onto other areas of college life. This can compound feelings of homesickness and loneliness. There is nothing worse than feeling lonely in the company of others.

Most colleges have channels for getting room reassignments. Sometimes these can be successful and other times, overcrowded campuses do not have resources for moving freshmen students around to other rooms or other residence halls. Not only that, but by the time you come to face the reality that things with this particular roommate are never going to work out, the deadline for asking for a reassignment may have passed. If you sense that your student is having trouble beyond what is reasonable, encourage him or her to seek a change early on before it becomes unrealistic.

For some, the prospect of figuring out the system for making a roommate change, or the potential for conflict when the existing roommate finds out, will be enough to allow your student to tolerate existing conditions. Resist the urge to step in and consult with the residence hall staff or the admissions office. This is not your problem. Your job is to listen and be supportive and empathetic, not to fix the problem (unless stepping in is warranted by an out of the ordinary situation).

When we attended the University of Nebraska freshman orientation, the student orientation crew performed a skit for parents and students. The skit was about two freshmen girls sharing a room. They both started out hating each other and being uncomfortable around each other. They each call their parents when the other one is out of the room and complain about their roommate. They hate each other's music and friends, and generally get on each other's nerves. Then one day, several weeks into the semester, one of the girls, in a fit of loneliness, has an emotional breakdown. The other roommate comes in and finds the poor girl in a pool of tears. Upon hearing the problem, the other roommate also confesses to being homesick. They start to talk, discuss their respective home lives, and sigh over all the things they miss. They realize they have a lot more in common than they first thought. They end up becoming tight friends.

While this may not play out in real life quite as neatly as it did in the skit, I thought the moral of the story made a lot of sense. Take the time to get to know your roommate, even if you do not like him or her at first. It takes time to get to know people, so give them a chance. Before you encourage your complaining, unhappy student to head off to the Residence Hall authorities and ask for a new roommate, encourage him or her to make a real effort to get to know the other person. Sharing a small space with a stranger is difficult on many levels, even if you like the other person. Changing roommates may help, but it is no guarantee that things will improve.

Residence Hall Life

Each residence hall has its own culture. The culture can change from floor to floor, as different floors are sometimes reserved for different groups. The Biology Learning Community may occupy the entire third floor of one residence hall, for example, and they may put on their own activities for Biology Learning Community students every weekend. Another floor may be reserved for non-biology students. Some residence halls may be co-ed, single sex, or reserved exclusively for foreign students or honors students. They are all different and have their own unique atmosphere suited to those who live in them.

Whatever the culture of your student's new residence hall, your student will be busy in the first few weeks of college trying to fit in and find his or her place among a new group of strangers who often have nothing in common beyond their age, where there dorm is, and their desire to go to college.

Perhaps your student chose that particular college because of its modernized housing facilities with individual rooms in village style condos and access to a Jacuzzi and a massage therapist. However, the chances are high that as a freshman, they did not qualify for this kind of housing. Most freshmen still end up sharing a room in a traditional, dormitory style residence hall with a single, communal bathroom for an entire floor full of students.

Robin Raskin, in his book *"Parent's Guide to College Life,"* sums it up nicely:

> *"One day they're hanging out in the comfort of their childhood bedrooms; the next they find themselves thrown in with a random group of strangers in a stark dorm setting where they're expected to live in peace and harmony."*

Privacy during the first year of college is a thing of your student's past. It simply will not happen. When you share a room with someone and a bathroom with a whole group of people, it is hard to keep secrets. This can be hard to handle for any student. Some people need to spend a lot of time in quiet solitude. Others may be more sociable, but still shy in nature, and may not be used to having everyone know everything about them all the time. If you are the kind of person who enjoys peace and quite and likes to spend time alone every now and then, it can be challenging to find solitude. There are students everywhere you go on campus. There are not many nooks where you can find a place for quiet reflection. It is even harder if it is cold outside and you are looking for a place that is not far to go, and offers warmth and shelter from the weather outside which is beginning to develop the first chills of autumn.

The Dining Hall

The trick to the dining hall experience on campus, according to Stu, is figuring out which one serves the best food and then arranging your life so you end up at that side of the campus at meal times. Quality and selection of food in dining halls can vary somewhat, partly depending on the student's expectations and personal culinary appetite and partly depending on the kitchen staff.

Most universities offer a choice of meal plans. The two-meals-a-day plan with a small allowance on the student card is friendlier for some students than the three-meals-a-day plan. You may think that setting up your student with three squares a day is the best thing you can do. But the reality is they probably will not eat in the dining hall three times a day. For one thing, most dining halls are not open every hour of every day, and may be closed completely over the holidays and on long weekends. On weekend mornings, many of them are not open for breakfast until 11 a.m. or so, when it almost lunch time. Most close by a certain hour in the evening, just before the period of the evening when campus social life really kicks in, homework due the next day finally gets attended to, and students have a tendency to work up a hearty appetite.

While you are peacefully sleeping in your bed, your

student may be making a run to the all-night hot wings store at three in the morning, having skipped lunch and dinner in the dining hall. He may never have time to step into the dining hall for an 8 a.m. breakfast because he sets his alarm for 8:45 a.m. to get to his 9 a.m. class. So do not stress over the meal plan. If you can save a few dollars by not purchasing a three-meals-a-day plan, it may be well worth considering. You can also consider applying some funds to a debit card. That way your student can use it in restaurants close to campus on weekends or assuage late night hunger pangs after the dining hall has closed by going across the street to the burger place. This can be a nice perk when he has to pull an all-nighter to get a psychology essay turned in on time.

Even if you have a more conservative student, or one of the rare ones that actually eats breakfast, and even if you absolutely know they will never consider eating hot wings at 3 a.m., it can be a nice break for them to eat off campus once in a while. Even the best dining halls become routine and boring after several straight weeks of nothing else to eat, and even the most conservative students eventually get bored with them or run into times they are closed.

The Recreation Center

Physical activity is a great stress reliever after the boredom of sitting in long, crowded classes. For a student who ends up with two hours to kill in the middle of the day, it can be a useful and beneficial way to settle the mind, fill up some time, and get the body ready for the next period of concentration. Some colleges include the recreation center fees in their basic fee structure and for others it is an additional expense. Either way, it is good value for the money, provided your student uses it. A student who uses the recreation center has found a constructive way to refresh his or her mind and body and will be in a good position to meet students of many disciplines who are like-mindedly indulging in healthy activity that is keeping them away from drugs, alcohol, and fraternity parties.

For students who like to run or keep fit outdoors, the recreation center is a great place to go when the weather is too cold or too hot and they do not feel like running outside. It is a place to get away from your room and can help you overcome homesickness or boredom when you cannot think of anything else to do.

Support from the Home Front

Even though your student may not always let you know when he has a problem, and may not tell you everything that is going on, it brings him comfort to hear from you. Staying in touch with your child is important even if he does not always reciprocate when you reach out to him. One nice way to do this is to send cards, letters or small packages. Most students have a mailbox and check it regularly, but do not often find real mail there. Most colleges do care packages as fund raisers. You may get a notice in the mail offering to send a care package to your student around exam time. Of course, there is a fee to cover the cost of the items being sent, but it can be a convenience if you are too busy to stop and put one together yourself, or if you are not sure of the best time to have it delivered. Whether you send a canned care package or your own, it is nice to do something to let your student know you are thinking of him. Even a small gesture, such as a pack of gum or a favorite candy bar can go a long way to helping him feel loved and a little less lonely.

Staying in Touch

Different people prefer different methods of communication. Ian never talks much when he is home, but he calls me every week to hear what is going on and find out news about his brothers. Stu is a great conversationalist and when he is here in person, he will engage me for hours at a time in a great debate or some lively chit-chat. But he never writes and he never calls when he is away from home. Sometimes I will e-mail him and ask him for a response — to which I get the trite reply, sometimes in text message format, *"Alive and well in Atlanta. Stop worrying Mom."*

I have learned to be content with the alive and well message and I understand that Stu needs to strike out on his own and do everything by himself. He is afraid of long lectures and unwelcome advice if he spends too long on the phone. More than that, he is afraid that the conversation will inevitably turn to his grades, which he would really prefer not to talk about at any time.

A lot of people recommend Instant Messenger (IM) as an

invaluable tool. If you do not already use IM, this may be the time to learn how to set it up and use it. Most parents say that a cell phone is also a must. One parent went to the length of setting up fixed times so as not to disturb or interrupt her student, every Wednesday and Sunday at 11 p.m. (remember students live on different schedules than the outside world). Most students sleep late on weekends, so unless you absolutely know that your student is different from most — do not call before noon on weekends, or at least, do not expect them to always pick up the phone.

These days, most students do not use the dorm room phone and do not even know the number, so a cell phone is almost a necessity. But if you cannot afford a cell phone plan, another option is to get an answering machine for the dorm-room phone. At least that way you can stay in asynchronous contact. You may occasionally catch your student in the room, but if not, you can let her know you are trying to reach her.

If you send e-mails, do not expect a reply. Even if students do not reply, they appreciate getting an e-mail. Students like to hear about what is going on at home. Focus on giving them news from home rather than asking them questions about how things are going. Tell them what new things you have purchased for the home, how your carrot crop did this year, or how their younger brother or sister is doing in school or sports.

If they do call with problems, be a listener, not a problem solver. Encourage them to think out solutions to their own problems and keep letting them know you are there if they need you. *The Georgia Tech Parents Handbook* recommends being available and supportive without being over-protective.

> *"Allow the students to make their own mistakes, and let them grow at their own pace."*

In an article published on the University of Nebraska Housing Web site, entitled "What Should Parents Expect From Their Student the First Few Weeks of Semester?" Ina Sivits Lurning advises parents to let students know that you trust their judgment (even if you do not).

> *"Trust is the single most important thing you can communicate to your son or daughter. Communicate your belief that they will make good choices. Over the years you have instilled in them values, beliefs, knowledge of your expectations, and the foundation for your current relationship. It's time to continue to build upon that foundation with the same level of trust and respect that you would like to receive from your student."*

The Nebraska Housing Web site goes on to remind us that students respond best when they feel we are interested and listening, and communicate less if they feel like they are being quizzed. Even though you think your questions are innocent, a lot of questions about schoolwork, grades, and what time they get to sleep at night will begin to sound like the third degree to your student. Remember most students do have a conscience, know your values, and may already be harboring some guilt that you would disapprove of their new lifestyle. So they start out on the defensive. It is almost impossible, however innocent your intentions, to ask a student "So how are your classes going?" without it sounding (in their mind) like the inquisition. It is their inner filter, not your outer demeanor that is at play here, so there is no need to take it personally.

CHAPTER 10

College Classes

Classes are the reason your student has gone to college. However, given the fact that in a lecture hall with 100 students and one professor, it is easy not to be missed, and given the multitude of other things to attend to once you start college, it is easy to understand how going to class has a tendency to drop down to the bottom of some students' list of priorities.

My sons frequently tell stories about students not attending class. Some get away with it. Most see drops in their grades. Some struggle with homework assignments for which they missed the background lecture. Some have below 2.0 GPAs. Many have lost their renewable scholarships after their first year in college because they were unable to maintain the required GPA.

When I attended the parent portion of freshman orientation at Georgia Tech, one of the topics talked about was how to help your student develop their priorities. I was impressed with the visual metaphor used to demonstrate how students are suddenly faced with a multitude of things to deal with that they have never had to deal with before. The presenter enlisted the participation of the parent audience to make his point. He asked volunteer parents to line up at both sides of the stage. At the left side of the stage, the parents were given balls of various different sizes. These balls represented all the things that students have to deal with after they leave the umbrella of their parents' home. The parents in this line were to throw the different balls rapidly at the parents on the right side of the stage. The parents on the right side of the stage were to come forward one by one and catch as many of the balls as they could.

The ball-throwing parents were doing a great job of hurling the balls, and the ball-catching parents were doing an equally spectacular job of catching them until the moment that the presenter stepped into the middle with a large basketball and threw it into a stream of smaller balls at the next unsuspecting parent waiting in the catching line. The volunteer catcher, confused by the onslaught of several balls at once, rushed at a small easy ball and missed the big ball.

The big ball represented academic work at the University. By catching the small ball, which was close and easy to catch, students often miss the big ball, which is the only ball they absolutely must catch.

The presenter laughed out loud, but continued to throw his large ball while the throwing-parents continued to throw their small balls. Balls were flying left and right into the audience as parents darted now after a tennis ball, now after a softball, missing all the balls. Finally, one parent stood stock still, letting all the balls fall to the floor until the presenter threw the basketball. He stepped forward calmly and with grace, held out his arms and caught the basketball. Everyone clapped.

The parent who caught the big ball stood in the middle of the stage, proudly holding it in his hands. *"I've done this before,"* he declared. *"I'm an alumnus."* He knew that the secret was to focus entirely on catching the large ball and let the small balls fall where they may. The small balls represent laundry, e-mail, instant messaging, partying, phone calls to mom and dad, and, in short, everything else that students deal with besides class. When there is time and energy, you catch the small balls; but when there is not, you focus on the big ball. It is the reason you are in college.

Throughout your child's high school career you probably caught a lot of the small balls, helping to take off the strain. You were the one arranging dental appointments, getting her to sporting events, reminding her of community service and other extra-curricular activities, and keeping her on track with homework. You fielded all the small balls so she could catch the large ball. Now you are not there and the small balls are whizzing by her head, distracting her, and causing her to lose focus.

Before your send your children off to college, be sure they have a clear vision of what their priority is. Let them know that the degree is the big ball, and it is only important to catch that one. Make sure they know how to ask for help when they get overwhelmed.

Listening to the Professor

We have all heard the sayings: "Give the customer what he wants" and "The customer is always right." When you are in philosophy class and you have a strong disagreement with the teacher's philosophy, and you are a teenager anxious to make your mark in the world, it can be difficult to remember that the teacher is your customer. If you want the teacher to give you a good grade, you must find out what he or she is looking for in your paper, and deliver it.

Now I am not saying you must compromise your values or your opinions or change the way you think about the world just to please a teacher. But the teacher has the power. The teacher grades the paper and no matter how strongly you believe in yourself, if you do not give the teacher what they are looking for, you will not get the grade. Part of the task of being in a class is to learn the subject and the other part is to figure out what the teacher wants from you. The second part is easy to overlook and can be the reason why some students do not do well in college.

Most college professors give out information, clues, and hints as to what they are looking for. Students who learn to tune into these clues, which can be subtle, tend to do better in class.

All students are different, and all professors are individuals and have their own unique styles of lecturing. Some colleges enforce a college culture in their teaching approach with goals and standards upheld uniformly across the teaching staff, and others do not. Some of your child's classes are likely to be large and impersonal, whereas others may be small and friendly. There will be various approaches to how tutoring or mentoring is offered and how easy it is to get in touch with the counselors or professors.

Even if you have drilled your student ahead of time to enroll for tutoring or to meet regularly with his professor, it can still be a pretty daunting task finding out how to do that and where the professor's office is located, times he is available, and so on. This is the big ball that it is sometimes easier not to catch while you are fielding smaller balls.

Here are some other points worth considering:

- At some time or another your student will probably encounter professors who do not resonate well with students and do not seem to give high grades no matter how hard students work.

- Math is generally much harder in college than in high school, even if your child took math at an honors level, and math is a pre-requisite to many disciplines, especially science and engineering.

- Calculus I is the primary reason many students choose to change majors and become arts majors rather than science majors. It is a "weeding out" class.

- Many students have trouble when it comes to mid-terms and final exams because the questions on the test do not seem to relate to what was taught in class.

- If you do not show up to class, you are not penalized. If you do not know the material, you are penalized. But you may not find out quite how much you do not know the material until it is too late to show up for class.

- Students over 18 do not have to share their grades with parents.

- Parents of students over 18 do not have to pay for school if their students will not share their grades with them.

- Some college students lie about their grades to their parents. Yes, even your student may be lying.

- Some students (especially boys) have trouble asking for help and see going to counselors or tutors as failure or weakness. Other students are intimidated by the process of going to see a counselor and may not ask for help when they need it.

- If your student has a renewable scholarship it is probably dependent on maintaining a certain GPA. If the GPA slips, the scholarship is not renewed.

Developing a Strategy

Stu has trouble with math, yet he wants to be an engineer. He knew math would be hard, but he thought taking chemistry in his first semester would be a fairly safe bet. However, he found the math to be difficult, even in chemistry class. He told me he studied hard for the chemistry exam and used his class notes and the recommended chapters of the book. But still, the questions on the final did not seem to relate to the topics he had covered in class. This is a common phenomenon at the college level. Students who are doing badly are not necessarily skipping class and forgetting to turn in their assignments. Some students are trying, but are really struggling with the material.

In high school, we are taught facts and encouraged to memorize them. In history, your student probably memorized plenty of names and dates. In college, you are supposed to learn to use facts to make deductions, correlations, and connections. In short you are learning how to think, not how to churn out memorized formulas. You are expected to develop and prove theorems, not learn them. This can be a shock to many students.

Most students take between 12 to 16 credits per semester (you are required to take a minimum of 12 to be considered a full-time student and to qualify for many scholarships). Sixteen credits translates to approximately 30 hours of classes in many cases, though hours may vary depending on whether labs are associated with the classes, whether the classes meet every day, and so on. In freshman year, if students attended freshman orientation, they probably received guidance from a counselor on how to combine a couple of electives with a couple of prerequisites for their major.

At some point before the semester is over, and before they know the outcome of their first semester grades, they will need to make decisions about what classes to take the following semester. They are going to have to make some strategy decisions:

- They may need to retake a class they think they may be failing if it is a prerequisite for their major.

- They may need to take an easy elective they may not need to bring up their GPA to maintain a scholarship.

- They may face the realization that their major is not, after all, what they want to focus on for the rest of their life and they may decide to switch majors.

As your student is weathering the ups and downs of the first semester grades, they are contemplating their options, sometimes confronting the possibility of failure, or realizing this is not what they want to do after all. Compounded with the pressures of freshman life in general and all they are dealing with in their first few months away from home, this can be an overwhelming time. In the back of their minds at all times is the thought of breaking the news, whatever it is, to you, their loving parent and source of college funding.

Declaring or Changing Majors

Changing majors can have implications regarding scholarships. A student may be receiving a music scholarship and decides he would rather study French, but the scholarship is not transferable. An engineering student with a scholarship from the School of Engineering may decide to switch to business management (a common occurrence following the first or second semester of calculus), but the engineering scholarship will be lost.

Yale University, among others, discourages students from declaring a major in their first year. Other colleges require that you at least declare a discipline, such as engineering, but do not require you to specify which particular engineering major you want to focus on. Some schools with narrow overall emphasis on arts or technical subjects will by default have limits on what your choices are if you decide to change majors.

At Yale University, on their sophomore page, an article entitled *"Choosing a Major"* embodies the Yale philosophy:

> *"Your choice of major should conform to your intellectual interests and preferences, which become clear only after you have looked into a variety of subjects and have sought faculty advice. The subjects you have studied in freshman year and the ones you choose in sophomore year should give you a sense of what engages your interest, makes good use of your talents, and satisfies you as an intellectual enterprise."*

The Penn State Web site has a good article on declaring a major, entitled *"Major Decisions"* (see the bibliography at the end of this book for more information). The article tells us that according to research conducted at Penn State and other organizations, up to 80 percent of students entering college do not know what they want to major in. What is more, *"up to 50 percent of college students change their majors at least once before graduation, and some change several times."*

Some undecided students strategize that if they choose nothing but electives, they can put off choosing a major until much later in their college career. However, this is not always a wise policy because often only certain electives are available for certain majors.

While it is an intellectually satisfying philosophy to try on various subjects and see how they fit, and there is no doubt that each of us at heart wishes our child to be happy in their chosen career field, as parents we see dollar signs in front of every change of course that our children embark on and wonder how we are going to take the money that we planned on spending on their four-year education and make it last six. This can make it hard for us to support them in their indecision and make us want to rush in and shake them up. But try to have patience as your student figures out what he wants to do. It is a big wide world out there — the choices are endless, and it can be a tough decision deciding what you want to do for the rest of your life.

Seeking Out Tutors

At most colleges, freshmen are assigned a personal

counselor to help keep them on track academically and help them navigate the maze of requirements and electives. The hope is that the counselor will help the student find the most efficient and satisfying path to meet their interests, and get a degree without running up five or six years of tuition bills. All they have to do is ask. *The Georgia Tech Parents Handbook* advises parents to *"Encourage your student to seek out tutors and be persistent."* This persistence is key because sometimes when an idea is new to you, you have to hear it over and over again from different sources before it begins to make sense to you. When a friend's boys were in college, they sometimes had difficulty asking for help. Tom's advice now is that college services are good. These are the experts who have helped thousands upon thousands of students and they have a clear understanding of what most students are facing and know how to help. Tom cautions that the hardest part is getting your student to ask for help. Even after they ask, they sometimes have difficulty understanding the importance of the advice they receive.

> *"Orientation, publications, and counselors are very helpful, BUT you have to ask questions and listen to the answers."*

Mid-Terms

Several weeks have passed and students are beginning to settle into college life. There is more of a familiar ring to it all than there was at the beginning, and they are starting to develop a sense of the new rhythm of their life. Just as things are starting to get on an even keel, they have to wrestle with mid-terms. This can be a rattling experience. Many students who sailed through high school barely studying for exams encounter a different experience taking exams at the college level. No longer subject to the rote memorization that sufficed in high school, questions on college exams sometimes do not even seem to be derived from the things learned in class. College professors often draw from background reading for exam material. Your student may or may not have invested time and money in these readings. Reading around your subject is rarely necessary in high school and its importance can often be completely overlooked by the unseasoned freshman student.

Those who may not have done as well as they wanted to on their mid-terms may be filled with self doubt at this point.

Once the first set of college exams are behind them, students have a much better understanding of what lies ahead and how academic work is going to be different from what they grew used to in high school. If you suspect your student is partying all night and not studying, that is one thing. It is sometimes hard to tell if your student is experiencing difficulty in studying and keeping up with material — they may not always tell you or express it in those terms. But try to remain positive as they wrestle with their new situation. In their parents' handbook, Georgia Tech recommends praising accomplishments regardless of how small they are. It is important to support students if you know they are trying: *"Their grades will not be all As so be ready to praise the C grade."*

Learning How to Study

If you have a reasonable communication channel with your child, it is quite an interesting exercise to discuss learning techniques. High school study tactics draw heavily upon rote memorization, but in college you have to learn to think for yourself. If your student is having trouble with math, in particular, or one of the sciences (that draw heavily on math) it may be as simple as learning how to study the material. Study techniques are not emphasized or taught in high school because high school subjects do not demand such a high degree of study.

Some subjects, like English and history, focus on essay writing and building an argument to support an opinion or theory. Other subjects, like music or French, are more intuitive and you tend to develop a "feel" for the subject rather than apply a specific technique to learn it. With intuitive subjects, you are either good at them or not. But subjects like math, physics, and chemistry, which depend heavily on solving equations, algebraic arithmetic, and calculus, need a different approach. You have to study the solution to a problem by going over and over the steps, with a piece of scratch paper and a calculator handy, and analyze how each step progresses to the next. This is not the same technique that you would use to prepare for a history assignment. The study technique to be successful at math is unlike any other subject. You have to develop an understanding of the theory of the solution, not just follow the calculations as they happen. You need to do this over and over again until you truly appreciate the approach to the solution. More often than not with math, a student is focusing on understanding the arithmetic and cannot always follow the progression of the problem well enough to adapt the approach to a similar problem, but one that has a slight twist or small difference.

A lack of ability in how to study math is more of an encumbrance to most students than the math itself. Stu repeatedly told me that he studied for the exam, and analyzed problems that he got wrong in class, but on the tests was unable to solve the problems that were presented.

Because math study techniques are not taught well in school (teachers who are brilliant at math are often reportedly poor at teaching the subject), you end up with one of the most complicated subjects, coupled with one of the least understood study techniques. These two things combine to compound the level of difficulty.

Add this to the leap in level of difficulty between high school math and college math, and mix in the fact that college freshmen are dealing with a change in lifestyle, an unbridled amount of free time, and an inordinate exposure to life's new experiences, and it is easy to see why this subject probably causes more problems for students than any other.

Dealing with Failure

Hopefully there will not come a point in your student's college career where they encounter failure rather than success. But failure does happen, and it can happen to the best of us at the worst possible time.

As parents, the reality is that we may not always be the first to know about it. The school will not tell you. Your student may be sullen and withdrawn, or irritable with your repeated questions about grades. Inside he will be attempting to deal with the situation by himself and figure out a strategy for redemption.

When you do find out, your immediate (and justifiable) reaction may be one of anger. If your student has been lying to you or withholding the truth, just remember that this is exactly why your student has not been up front with you in the first place.

Have a Plan B

If failure causes financial pressure because of extending the number of years in college, or loss of a scholarship, there are several ways to mitigate the situation. It can help a student if he knows the expectation from the beginning. Perhaps you make it clear that attendance at a certain, expensive school is contingent upon maintaining a certain grade point average and if the GPA drops, the student must register at a local community college or local state school until the grade is brought up. You can make this clear in a matter-of-fact way. Just a clear statement of fact.

If a scholarship is lost and you do not have the money to make up the lost tuition, you can make it clear immediately that the student either has to find his own money to cover tuition or switch schools.

Many times the situation is not that bad. A lost grade or two can be made up if the other grades are reasonable. Retaking one class is often sufficient for a student to work harder in other classes to avoid a similar situation. If the student was struggling with the material, retaking it one more time can make all the difference.

Before you lay down an ultimatum, have the patience to listen to your student's own mitigation plan. Sometimes your student can get good advice from a counselor that you may not be in a position to offer. At Georgia Tech, they offer "freshman forgiveness" for students who do badly in their first two semesters. If you retake a class in your freshman year at Georgia Tech and do better the second time, the first grade will be thrown out and is not factored in your GPA. This level of support from a college can be helpful.

If all else fails, there are plenty of people in the world who took full-time jobs and worked their way through college. A friend reports that both his boys dropped out of college by sophomore year because they struggled with developing good study habits. They eventually partnered in real estate development and today enjoy a better income than their father, who has a master's degree in engineering. Do not give up on your children. Wait and see what they are able to accomplish despite failing a college class or dropping out altogether.

CHAPTER 11

Learning Independence

Obtaining a college degree is the primary reason for going to college. But another reason for leaving home and going away to college is to help young people transition successfully from childhood into adulthood. Before our children leave home, we teach them how to use the washing machine and drill them on the importance of maintaining a healthy balance in their bank account. It is much harder to teach them emotional independence — things like how to survive loneliness — how to solve just about any problem that might arise.

Far From Home

When Stu left to go to Atlanta (a three and half hour plane ride away), it was only feasible to bring him home for the major holidays: Thanksgiving, Christmas, and Spring Break. This meant that when he left for college in mid-August, he did not get his first trip home until the end of November for Thanksgiving. It never even occurred to me to try and bring him home during fall break, which was only a couple of days, and occurred in October. I also decided against visiting him during

Parents' Week, which was in September, because after traveling around to several colleges during the previous year and paying out of state tuition for the first semester, I had no resources left to fund the trip. In retrospect, this was a long time alone in a far away city, and during those four months, Stu learned to deal with a variety of problems by himself.

When he first left for college, we were in touch fairly regularly because we had a lot of details to work out regarding his lost luggage. We passed casual commentary on how college was going, but Stu always seemed to be in a hurry to get off the phone and rush off to some social activity or another, so I kept my conversations light and short and assumed he was having a rip-roaring social life. I hoped that class was going well but I could not get much information out of him on that subject.

One Saturday in October, the phone rang. Stu was calling to tell me it was fall break and most of his friends had gone away for the long weekend. Only one or two of his friends, because they happened to be foreign students, remained in the residence hall. Stu chatted for over an hour, about this and that, about what he missed and what his life was like. It was the first time I heard what things were really like for him in college.

Stu's luggage had been lost when he arrived at Georgia Tech. We hastily replaced some items immediately, and he made do without many of his belongings until they were eventually found and delivered. I guess he had things pretty hard until the last of his boxes arrived, two months into the semester. He had a rockier start to college than most students. Hearing him discuss out loud his options for spending his free time that week, I felt bad that I had not even thought about bringing him home for fall break.

Ian, Stu's older brother, had made frequent trips home during his first semester because he was still wearing his braces and needed occasional dental checkups. I always thought of these trips as necessities and did not realize how much they were helping Ian — away from home for the first time, but able to check back in at home, even for a brief overnight stay.

Coming Home for Thanksgiving

I know of students who did not go home for Thanksgiving during their first semester at college. Most were attending college on the other side of the country, and I cannot blame their parents because I know how incredibly hard it is to pay for everything and still have enough left to keep your home going. However, if it is reasonably possible for you to do so, you should try and bring your student home sometime during the first semester. They need and benefit from it. If you have not had the opportunity to visit with them or bring them home in September or October, then Thanksgiving may be the first opportunity.

Some campuses do not stay open at Thanksgiving. You hear stories through your children of students who had to stay in a motel for a couple days because they could not afford to go home and the campus closed for the long weekend. Your heart goes out to these students, who, if they are freshmen, are probably aching for a trip home. But as a struggling parent putting two children through college at the same time, I can also sympathize with the parents. It is not easy to come up with the money to fly your student home several times per semester.

When something is difficult, whether it is learning to play the piano, studying a math problem, or learning to live on your own, taking a break from it and going back to it somehow makes it seem easier and more familiar after the break.

When Stu arrived home at Thanksgiving, his dad picked him up at the airport and dropped him off at my house. His smile as he walked through the door stretched across the entire width of his face. He just stood there in the doorway for a few minutes, with his duffle bag in one hand and his laptop in the other, moving his head from side to side, looking around at his home, and beaming. It was heartwarming. It made me wish I had been able to bring him home earlier in the semester.

I will admit that the experience he was having in college by Thanksgiving time was different, and much happier, than the experience he was having the first two or three weeks of college, but it still felt good to him to come home for a break, even though it turned out to be no more than two and a half days he was actually here.

You may think it is just a few short weeks from Thanksgiving to Christmas. But it is worth the trip home if you can manage it, especially in that first year. That brief sojourn with friends and family can provide the needed strength of spirit to return to college life and buckle down for final exams.

Random Acts of Independence

As much as we complain about the times that our children do not meet our high expectations, there are times when they outdo themselves. I remember catching myself once when the children were all small. They were messing around, giggling, and carrying on. For whatever reason that day I was feeling tired and frustrated and found myself getting into it with one of them. I caught myself yelling at my pre-teen "Why don't you just stop acting like a kid," to which he replied, of course, totally straight-faced and deadpan "Because I am a kid." I felt duly put in my place.

When our children turn 18, they are no longer children, but we still cannot expect of them all of the things we would expect of an adult who is older and has several years experience living on their own.

I have to remind myself of this every now and again. One day when all the children were home for Christmas break, I took myself off to the library for some peace and quiet. They have wireless Internet at my local library and I nestled myself and my laptop into a booth so I could quietly get some work done. Pretty soon my cell phone rang. It was Stu doing his laundry with a question about which laundry soap to use. Anxious to avoid a lengthy public conversation with him in the library, I quickly answered his question and hung up. If I would have stayed on the line a little longer I may have avoided coming home to find that all my delicates had been lovingly transferred, by Stu, from the washing machine into the dryer. The dryer, in turn, had been expediently cranked up to high for the fastest possible drying of said delicates to make room, in the most efficient manner, for Stu's jeans.

My oldest son had never regularly done his own laundry at home. Even though he appeared to have periodically kept up with it while he was away at college, I was not expecting him to accomplish his laundry while he was staying at my house. It was not that I was not eager to encourage his new found independence, I simply had not given it much thought. I had no way of knowing that my second son would be eager to flaunt his new skill on his first extended trip back home. He fully intended to be proactive in doing his own laundry. Furthermore, I had no insight into the fact that this would occur while I was away from home and had left my most valuable (and shrinkable) clothing items at risk in the washer.

My delicates, which had never before seen the inside of a dryer, were duly shrunk into the next size down. I came home to find them bundled and scrunched into a laundry basket while the dryer was humming and thumping its merry way through a load of size 36 blue jeans and extra large Led Zeppelin t-shirts. It was hard to lay blame or be upset with a male child who was willingly taking on the mundane responsibilities of adult life without any prompting, cajoling, or forcing on my part.

But be aware that the years between young adult and mature, experienced adult also have pitfalls along with the rewards. I learned when my boys were small that if you wanted any help around the house you have to refrain from any kind of criticism and accept childish, imperfect work at face value. In addition, you have to praise if any effort at all has been invested in the task. A small task that takes 30 seconds to complete is often a mighty accomplishment to a small child. In the same way, completing an unsolicited act of responsible adulthood is, for a teenager, a monumental accomplishment and requires inordinate amounts of praise to foster self-confidence and continued interest. Beware of criticizing, however kind your intentions, for fear of scaring off your young adult.

In the case of doing laundry, it pays to remember how many of your own clothes you ruined (and still may occasionally) while you were mastering the task. Just because you now perform flawlessly while your teenager does not, it is not the best reason to retain the task and reduce their opportunity for learning. While at home, your student will be anxious, at least on a sub-conscious level, to demonstrate their new skills to you. Remember to praise them and reward their attempts at independence as they learn the skill, rather than impart advice to them or give them "constructive feedback" on the task.

Remember when you hung their pictures on the refrigerator even though you could not tell whether they had painted a house or a dog? You never had to tell them that a dog has four legs, a head, and a tail, whereas a house has windows and a roof. They knew that all along and just had trouble expressing it creatively with crayons. Learning independence is not much different from learning to color inside the lines. Most of us eventually master it. All it takes is a little practice and encouragement.

Buying Soap, Deodorant, and Other Boring Supplies

Do you remember the first time you came face-to-face with the reality of paying income tax? Or the first time you had to spend a large chunk of your income on a home maintenance project or an unexpected medical bill? It is a sure sign of impending adulthood when you are called upon to budget for life's mundane and boring necessities rather than spending your hard earned money entirely on fun. Stu's first encounter with the cold, hard fact that adulthood is not just being able to drink legally and buy your own lighter fluid was probably harder than most.

Stu left the dry, moderate climate of Colorado for the hot, humid climate of the South. The day we arrived in Atlanta, Georgia in the middle of August for the beginning of his freshman year, it was 100 degrees with 100 percent humidity. This was not what we were used to. As I mentioned earlier, Stu was without most of his luggage. Expecting his boxes to be delivered the next day, Stu had traveled light. That meant he had not packed a toothbrush, soap, deodorant, or a change of underwear.

"Not even one pair of underwear?" I asked in horror.

"I thought I would just wing it until

tomorrow morning." His innocent faith in
the shipping company was disarming.

I had packed him one sheet and a small travel pillow in our carry-on luggage. These two items, along with his iPod, were all he would have possession of as he ventured off for his first night alone on campus. I could not let him go without a toothbrush, so we hiked to the far end of campus where there was a drugstore. I bought him some travel-sized basics. I had already spent most of my life savings on the first semester's tuition, room and board, and now this trip halfway across the country. I was feeling a little poor and sorry for myself. I mention this to explain my frame of mind when I suddenly found out that I had to come up with funds for still more supplies:

"You can double up the shampoo as
soap since it is just for one night."

So I left him with these items in his possession as he ventured off for his first night alone on campus:

- 1 travel size deodorant

- 1 travel size shampoo

- 1 toothbrush

- 1 travel size toothpaste

- His iPod

- 1 bed sheet

- 1 small travel pillow

- And the clothes on his back

I think he may have had a book with him as well.

Anger and confusion clouded my judgment on the following day when I found that half his luggage was lost, and I consequently forgot to pick up a proper bar of soap to leave with him. I advised him to pick one up for himself at the convenience store next time he was in there to buy soda. I bought him new underwear, a towel, new socks, new t-shirts, and some shorts, but I figured the travel-sized toiletries would tide him over until the boxes arrived on the following day. But the boxes did not arrive the next day.

Stu called several times during the first few weeks of college, mostly to discuss the situation with the lost boxes. He reported a rash on his arms and legs, which we determined to be heat rash. After a few weeks, one of the missing boxes finally arrived. This was the box with his soap, deodorant, and other necessities. A week later, he called again.

"How's the rash?"

"It's gone now. Surprising how quickly it cleared up after the soap arrived."

Stu, who turned 18 three weeks after college started, had been using his shampoo in place of soap for about a month. Ever optimistic that the semester supply of soap, so carefully packed for him by his attentive mom, would arrive any day, it seemed futile to spend precious resources on something as mundane as soap. After all, I had made so much of him sticking to his budget.

Due to excessive usage in the first month, the bottle of shampoo he had been using ran out fairly early in the semester. He called to express how annoying it was to spend money on soap and shampoo when he would rather buy DVDs or iTunes and Chipotle burritos.

"Welcome to adulthood." I could have bought a Lexus for cash for what it was costing me to send my son to an out-of-state college for one year.

CHAPTER 12

Handling Problems

Watching our children grow up and pull away from us is harder than we think it is going to be. The temptation is to pull them back or spend long sleepless nights worrying about them once they confess a problem to us. When they call us just to say hi, we give them advice. When they come home for the holidays just to visit with us, we give them more advice.

Ian's advice to parents of college students on giving advice goes as follows:

> *"Don't give your kids advice unless they ask for it, because they're probably eager to try things their own way. Even though you probably want to help them, they have to figure things out on their own."*

You have known your child for 18 years and you know whether they like to complain and vent out loud or whether they prefer to suffer in silence when life is going wrong. However, since they left home and went off to college you feel a little more out of touch. Perhaps the phone calls and e-mails have been sporadic and you are not sure how they doing. They have mentioned a couple of things in passing and you did not worry too much about it because you figured they would let you know if something serious was going wrong.

At the same time you want to be a good parent and you are trying your best to take a non-interfering role and encourage them to sort out their own problems.

Then you get a phone call and you realize they are dealing with a problem. Perhaps your student is seriously ill or had some terrible kind of accident. It happens. What do you do now? Unless the problem is something out of the ordinary, resist the temptation to drop everything and get on the next flight. Do not even list off the steps that you would take to solve the problem right away. Give students the opportunity to use you as a sounding board and explore their own solutions to the problem. Do not worry if the solution they come up with is not the one you would choose. Learning how to solve problems at this stage of the game is more important than coming up with the ideal solution. Besides, your child is an individual with his own personality, and even after he becomes a seasoned problem solver, the solution he picks may or may not be the solution you would describe as ideal for yourself.

The idea of letting your children solve their own problems in their own way can be harder on fathers than on mothers. A man's natural inclination when faced with a problem is to come up with a solution as quickly as possible. It is hard to take a back seat and watch your child make mistakes, but as long as nothing life-threatening is at stake, this is the best way for them to learn.

Getting Sick

Watching our children suffer, whether through illness or hardship, is the hardest part of parenting. It is hard on our children, too, to be away from us when they are in pain. In the book, *I'll Miss You Too*, by Margo Woodacre and her daughter, Steffany Bane, Steff admits to feeling vulnerable when she was sick:

> *"The times I missed my parents the most were when I wasn't feeling well physically or emotionally."*

As new parents, it comes as a shock that our time, once our own, now belongs almost entirely to our newborns. We get up with them for feedings during the night, and we comfort them through colic and nightmares. We stay up with them when they have a fever and spend long nights in the emergency room when they are sick or hurt. We get up at four in the morning to clean the carpet when they throw up, and we take time off work to nurse them through a bout of strep throat. It is our job as parents, after all, to look after our children. Nursing a child through sickness is a fundamental and primary duty of parenthood.

By the time they leave home, we have been trained across 18 years to tune in on their ailments, their little coughs and colds, and their serious illnesses. As mothers, we see it as our primary job in life to make them comfortable, make a fuss over them, and bring cups of hot chocolate with lots of marshmallows and homemade chicken soup. As fathers, we strive to protect them from anything that can hurt or injure them, and we build up our castle around them to protect them from the big bad world.

So when they call from the other end of the country, with weak, squeaky voices and signs of congestion, it is all we can do not to hop on the next plane out.

When Ian completed freshman year and spent his first summer back home, I realized how much he had grown to love running. He would go out every day on his run. One day, we happened to be talking about sports injuries and he mentioned his knee.

"What about your knee?"

"Well, one day I was running and I sort of hurt it, so I stopped running for a few days."

I could not get much more out of him. I asked him whether he went to the doctor. After all, knee injuries are fairly common for runners, and they can sometimes be serious.

A week or so later, I was walking past his room and I happened to notice a big black leg brace on the floor of his room. Clearly, his injury had been a lot more serious than he had cared to tell me. For Ian to go out and buy himself an actual leg brace, he must have been pretty worried about it.

When your children, especially boys, are sick, they are not always going to tell you. As children grow up, they try to deal with their problems themselves. The only thing you can do is support them when they need you, and leave them alone when they do not. After all, you do not want them to need you long into adulthood. It is good that they are learning to deal with their problems themselves. Make sure they have medical insurance and understand their coverage.

Stu went to a large campus. At home he had his own, air-conditioned car and drove himself wherever he needed to go. At college he was not allowed to bring his car during the first semester of freshman year. He went to a place where he had to walk for miles every day on a huge campus in 100-degree heat. In one infrequent phone call, he happened to mention that the blisters on his feet had cleared up.

> *"Blisters, what blisters?"*

> *"Yeah, I got these really big blisters on my feet from walking all over campus, but do not worry — they are all healing over."*

I asked him if he needed a new pair of walking shoes, but he preferred to keep the pair he had since they were now broken in. In his new environment, and completely unused to doing so much walking in excessive heat, Stu had been wrestling a bad case of heat rash and crippling blisters in his first few weeks of college. He mentioned the rash mostly, I think, because he needed advice as to what to put on it, but he never mentioned the blisters on his feet until it was too late for me to do anything.

He later recounted how grown-up it made him feel to go to the drugstore and buy his own medications. He bought some allergy medicine and some cream for the rash. That was before he discovered that using soap in the shower was also a pretty good cure.

Serious Illness

Joy's daughter, Heather, went to school in a small college town a couple of hundred miles away from home. She was not doing brilliantly in college and Joy had been practicing a little tough love to get her to take responsibility. In response, Heather had taken on a part-time job and was struggling to bring up her grades. She and Joy talked fairly frequently by phone and by instant messenger. Heather preferred instant messaging and e-mail, generally only telephoning when something was wrong. Right away Joy was nervous when she got Heather's phone call. Heather called Joy to complain that she was not feeling well. She complained of a fever and chills and a serious pain in her side. Joy's insurance did not cover Heather where she was going to school, so she told her daughter to go to an emergency care facility. The emergency care doctors could not pinpoint the illness. Eventually, after several days of becoming progressively worse, Heather ended up in the emergency room at the local hospital suffering from a serious kidney infection. Joy made the two-hour trip to the college and stayed over until her daughter was released from the hospital and well on her way to recovery. Heather spent a total of five days in the hospital.

> *"It was very, very scary! I can't imagine something like this happening when a child is out-of-state and too far away to get to them."*

When Joy was staying in Grand Junction with her daughter, she had plenty of time to observe her daughter's lifestyle up close and personal. Heather was working to support herself, as well as managing a full class load, yet she had no transportation and was begging rides from friends and roommates. Joy realized several things from this experience. She realized that she needed to offer some practical help to Heather and gave her a used car to help her get around more easily. She also encouraged her to move out of the house where she was staying with several other girls who were not pulling their weight in terms of keeping the place clean. Joy reported that beyond being messy, the place was unhygienic. Heather found another living arrangement with some new people who were better friends and better at keeping the house in order so that Heather was able to better look after herself and stay healthy. A year later, Heather was thriving. Her grades were up, she was more confident, and was well on her way to graduating.

I hesitated in providing this example, because in cases when tough love is necessary to get a child through a hard spot, you cannot just give in and give up or the strategy will backfire. It can be just as dangerous to step into a situation, from the perspective of getting your student to take responsibility for a situation, as it can be to stand back. On the other hand, you cannot just drop a child off in the deep end of life without a life raft and hope that they sink or swim. Their chances of success are much greater if you have given them a few tools, a few coping strategies, and yes, even perhaps a car or some money.

Certainly, it is always a tough decision and a fine line knowing when to remain strong for their sake and when to buckle and provide more money and more support to our children. Stories like this one make us vulnerable to giving into our children so we do not end up guilt-ridden when bad things happen. Not all situations are going to lead to hospitalization or near-death experiences. After 18 years of looking into your child's eyes to learn the truth, it is incumbent on us as parents of young adults to look for new ways to clue into the reality of their situations and determine when a situation is grave and when it is just difficult.

Medical Insurance

It sounds so nebulous to say that you will develop a feel for when to step in and when to step aside. Unfortunately, the art comes with practice and experience. The skill is honed from watching how you react and how your child reacts when certain things happen and how well they deal with those things and how well you deal with those things. Hopefully they deal better and better over time and you are called on to deal less and less. But one thing many parents have learned the hard way from personal experience is that it pays to make sure your student has adequate health insurance. This is something they are unlikely to know about or be able to prepare for on their own.

Whether or not they pay their own tuition or buy their own books, health insurance is an issue that most students feel they do not need to be concerned with themselves. Indeed, most financial matters are your worry in the first few years of college, not theirs. This is the case for the vast majority of students, and your student, by osmosis, will assume the beliefs of the majority. While your student sees it as his right to determine his own religious beliefs, choose his own major and his own hair color, and pay for his own tattoos, he will make the sweeping assumption that the matter of her health care insurance is squarely in your capable hands and pocket book.

One parent reports being grateful that she paid the Student Health Fee. Her daughter tore her ACL playing intramural soccer and was unable to drive home for Thanksgiving. Luckily, she was able to get on the spot care from the university clinic.

Another admits to wishing he had taken medical insurance through the school because his out-of-state policy did not cover some services that required special care off campus. Instead, he had to bring his son home for medical care. The cost of multiple trips home can far exceed the cost of additional medical insurance.

Most universities offer two types of coverage. One is a relatively low fee that covers basic visits to the health care facility. This at least provides for a preliminary diagnosis. After that, you have to pay or bill your regular insurance for any treatment. The second type is full medical coverage, at a slightly higher price, that covers your student as long as they are enrolled at the college. This type of insurance can run around one or two thousand dollars per year. It may sound like a lot on top of what you are already paying, but if your insurance is inadequate, consider the real cost you will be faced with if something does come up that requires treatment. During the course of four years, there is a real chance that something might.

Stu pays the fee for basic services. We reaped the benefit of this expense in his first semester. While horsing around in his residence hall one weekend, he was challenged by a fellow resident to jump over some boxes that were left in the hallway for an ill-defined reason. Stu was a linebacker in high school, not a track athlete. Nonetheless, he rose to the occasion. He cleared the boxes in a single bound, and hurtled downward with the full force of his 230 pounds into the doorway of his dorm room, stubbing his toe against the door jamb. The pain over the course of the next two days was enough to send this ex-football player to the university health center. Several X-rays later he was diagnosed with a broken toe. You never know what is going to happen once they get out on their own.

If your child is normally covered under your health insurance, you should take the time to find out what will happen if something happens in the college area. Is there a provider in the region that operates under your health care insurance? If something happens (like a broken bone or an infectious disease) that requires regular visits to the doctor and you do not have a provider in the neighborhood, you may have to pay a higher co-pay, pay everything from your own pocket, or alternatively, bring your student home regularly for treatment (which may incur further expense).

Mistakes

The University of Nebraska Parent Handbook reminds us:

> *"Learning how to manage a mistake will contribute to your student's ability to handle challenges throughout the rest of his or her life."*

It is important to develop a somewhat Zen-like approach to watching your son or daughter make mistakes. You can offer help and advice when you see things coming and your child may or may not choose to follow it. Even the best heart and most loving son or daughter will want to experiment with their own freedom and try their hand at managing their own life. But that does not mean everything will go perfectly.

Making life decisions can be hard work and requires a lot of practice. However, in return for your patience and understanding, it is not unreasonable to expect your child to take responsibility for their mistakes.

Do not feel you have to rush in and fix everything that

goes wrong. You will often be surprised and entertained as well as fiercely proud of how your child resolves issues and problems. Listening carefully, being supportive, and praising their efforts whether or not they turn out the way they intended are important strategies in helping your child adjust to adulthood. Remember when they first learned to put their own shoes on and more often than not they would put them on the wrong feet? But they do not do that now that they have mastered the skill.

Sarah Schupp, CEO of University Parent Inc., specializes in guides for parents visiting their children at college. Her Web site is **http://www.universityparent.com.** She gives the following advice for parents as their children embark on a college career:

> *"Provide your student with resources for success, support them, and be there as a guide, but do not make choices or decisions for them. College is a time to learn and to experience failure and success."*

There is nothing wrong with helping them if they ask for help. But help can take many forms. It is not necessary to give them all the steps for solving a problem. You may just point them to the right resources. Point them in the direction of a campus resource, for example, but let them look up the contact information on the campus intranet. Tell them what you would do, by all means, but do not expect them to do the same things as you would do. Expect them to experiment with their own approach and be supportive of the way in which they solve the problem.

Sex, Drugs, and Alcohol

If you are like most parents, one your biggest worries when your child goes to college is how they will deal with the readily available drugs and alcohol on campus. Information found at (**http://www.day.colostate.edu/ parents.asp**), Colorado State University's Web site, reminds us that students do not encounter drugs and alcohol for the first time in college. Unless your child has been subject to an extremely sheltered upbringing, there is a high probability that they have already said no multiple times to offers of drugs and alcohol. The average age that children first encounter these things is between 10 and 14 years of age. CSU states:

> *"The good news is that if your emerging adult has already safely navigated making responsible choices regarding alcohol or drug use, they will continue to do so. "*

Note that they also caution:

> *"Likewise, if your student has already had difficulty with substance abuse or irresponsible choices, they are likely to continue to do so or increase the frequency of negative behaviors."*

These statistics are not meant to alarm you or put you

off your guard. Rather, they are a reminder that drugs and alcohol are part of life and a part of adulthood. If we expect our children to take responsibility for their own lives and allow them to make their own way in the world, we must develop trust in their ability to overcome the vices and temptations of life in the same way we have overcome them ourselves.

Some parents are practical about alcohol and take a philosophical approach. If they go to college, they will drink, they will be confronted with drugs, and they will have sex. Better make sure they know how to deal with these things than expect them to resist all of life's vices for the rest of their days. As the commercials say, talk to your children about sex, drugs, and alcohol. Do it regularly, and start when they are young.

Money Problems

Money is one of those religious topics that most parents feel they have to step in and help with, whether or not the student has demonstrated money management skills. For most of us, there is simply not enough money available for college in the first place, without running the risk of wasting a lot of it in the process of learning how to manage it.

My cautious and conservative oldest son manages money well by not spending it. With him, I work on investment strategy so he can learn to leverage the money in his bank account by earning interest on it. My second son is more of a spendthrift. There are so many things in life he cannot seem to live without.

Stu opened a local bank account in Georgia so he would have access to cash, and he maintains another account in his hometown in Colorado, of which I am joint custodian. We moved $750 from his Colorado account to his Georgia account when he opened and applied $350 in funds to his Buzzcard (Georgia Tech's student debit card). That meant he had about $1100 in the middle of August when the semester began. He had a two-meals-a-day plan at the dining hall, plus his BuzzFunds to spend how he chose, be it food or other supplies. Stu rarely eats breakfast so two square meals constitutes a full day's meal plan, as a general rule. I paid for all his textbooks. All he had to do was buy himself drinks and snacks for a few months. I left him with some food and drink supplies on hand, including a generous supply of powdered sport drink mix. I thought $1100 would more than cover his needs for one semester.

I began to suspect that something was amiss shortly before Thanksgiving when I noticed that he was increasingly using his Colorado bank ATM card. Since I was joint custodian on that account, I could watch the activity. I had no insight into his Atlanta account.

Around that time, just before Thanksgiving, I missed a vital clue. He had withdrawn cash from his Colorado account and paid the mandatory additional transaction fee for drawing on an out-of-state bank. After Thanksgiving, I noticed he was increasingly using his Colorado ATM card, which I thought was strange. I suspected that he had drained his Atlanta account.

When he came home at Christmas I asked him how the

money was doing in his Atlanta account. He lied and said it was fine. Finally, on the way back to Atlanta to begin spring semester, I was able to get him to confess that the money was all spent. Doing post analysis on his spending, the $1100 probably ran out a little before Thanksgiving. Even so, with no real expenses being absolutely necessary, and knowing he had burned through his whole year's allowance in a few short months, he continued to rack up additional expenses.

Below is the actual capture from his Colorado bank account record after Thanksgiving and before I put a stop to his wanton spending. In the account below I was thoughtful enough to leave out additional expenses that he incurred by buying Christmas presents for his family (which were slight by the way) and one other expense that I was not sure he would want exposed to the world! But for someone already out of money and with no real need of food or any necessities, these are the expenses that Stu felt he could not live without, even though he knew he was well over budget:

BANK STATEMENT SNAPSHOT		
Date	Purchase	Price
12/20	Chipotle	$ 6.28
12/18	Ammo for rifle	$ 53.53
12/17	Music CD	$ 12.95
12/15	Chipotle	$ 22.19
12/14	Subway tickets	$ 3.50
12/14	Subway tickets	$ 3.50
12/12	Wingnuts	$ 5.91
12/03	Drugstore	$ 8.81

BANK STATEMENT SNAPSHOT		
Date	**Purchase**	**Price**
12/03	Supermarket	$ 17.49
11/26	Rifle	$ 97.64
11/26	Cold Stone Creamery	$ 7.28
11/26	Chinese Wok	$ 9.56
GRAND TOTAL		$285.18

All told, Stu burned through over $1600 in his first semester on a budget of about $725. In contrast, his brother, who is frugal by nature, but preceded Stu to college and therefore set my expectation, spent somewhere in the neighborhood of $350 in his first semester. Ian did have a three-meals-a-day plan, but we gave Stu that option also and he said he did not intend to eat that much and would rather have the cash to indulge his rather serious Chipotle habit.

When Stu admitted on his way back to college in January that his money had, in fact, run out as I suspected, I spent a lot of time soul searching after I said goodbye to him. I was angry that he had lied to me. His dad and I decided it was time for some tough love. At that rate of money burn, Stu, who earned $500 the summer after graduation, was going to run out of money faster than he could earn it. He had $2500 left in his Colorado Account and that was all the spending money he had for the foreseeable future.

I sent him an e-mail while he was still en route back to Atlanta. I tallied up what he had spent, told him what was left and told him he could transfer $300 for the semester to add to his Spring Semester Buzz Funds ($265). The rest I would shelter so he could not access it. I gave him one day's notice so he would not panic and think he had been robbed.

The next day at dawn I got up and moved his money via an electronic transfer out of his account into my own savings account.

He was shocked when I showed him the grand total of what he had spent. Having money in different accounts made it hard for him to accurately tally how much he was spending. In his mind he had only spent $750. He discounted his BuzzFunds because they did not seem like "real" money and he did not count the money he had spent from his Colorado account because in his mind he was only using it occasionally for small items. But those small items added up to more than he expected.

The way I handled Stu's money issue goes against my personal philosophy of letting children figure out their own way in life as long as it is not life-threatening. That is because college funds are in limited supply in my household and need to be safeguarded. In addition, I have no desire to see my son graduate college with $80,000 worth of student loans to pay off. So I guard the money closely and believe in spending only what is necessary. When I see the pot in jeopardy of depletion, I feel like I have to rush in and mediate the situation.

If you are lucky and money is not a problem for you, the better way is undoubtedly to let the student find out the hard way that when money runs out, the rough part of life kicks in. This may yet happen in Stu's case, we do not know. But I will do my best to ensure it happens later rather than sooner.

I think taking control of Stu's finances was a big kick in the rear for him. When he saw that I was prepared to take measures to mitigate the situation, he rallied and put himself on a budget. I assured him that once I had confidence his ability to manage his own money he would get it all back. He will probably never be frugal like Ian, but everyone should be capable of learning to manage on a budget.

CHAPTER 13

Mars and Venus in College

Differences in behaviors and outlooks on life between the sexes become apparent in children at a young age. A boy may be inclined to run around making a lot of noise and displaying aggression while playing with his peers, whereas a girl may be inclined to sit in a corner pursuing a quiet project or playing with dolls. Men tend to look outward toward the world and like to solve their own problems, whilst women tend to be relationship builders and like to talk over their problems with others. A mother who has not heard from her son in some time is likely to worry when she gets no news, good or bad, from her student. A father whose daughter calls every week to discuss a new problem will fight the urge to rush down to the college to fix everything for her.

Girls tend to take care of themselves and their necessities and do not mind spending money on cosmetics, toiletries, and the rest. But boys tend to be minimalists. If they do not have something that girls may consider necessary, boys will do without it.

When my boys left for college, I packed them as many of life's boring necessities as I could think of. Shampoo, deodorant, laundry soap — I tried to think of all the annoying things that would soak up their hard-earned money. My goal was not to equip them for the whole semester, but rather to buy one of everything I thought they would need. Then as it ran out, they could simply replace it. This removed the burden of having to think up the fact that they needed it in the first place. I deeply suspected that they would both do without something like laundry soap rather than buy it, if they possibly could. The mother in me cringed at the thought of them doing without the things that make day-to-day life go more smoothly, like soap and deodorant.

When I sent them care packages, I tucked in things like toothbrushes and toothpaste. I figured they would probably never replace their toothbrush themselves no matter how worn out it became. With girls, you do not need to worry about these things so much. Girls tend to take care of themselves and spend money on the things they need, which is not to say that you should not occasionally treat girls to these things. But for a girl, receiving free toothpaste is a treat, whereas a boy may not even look at it as that.

Even though it is more economical to buy a huge bottle of shampoo, I knew that it would not be easy for the boys to take it back and forth to the shower. I knew that even though they had a shower basket they were highly unlikely to use it. So I bought two small bottles of shampoo. Stu liked to use conditioner because he wore his hair long, so I bought a small bottle of leave-in conditioner because he could keep it in his room and would not have to cart it back and forth to the shower room. Logistics of this kind are important to boys who do not put forth any unnecessary effort in the area of personal hygiene and would rather place hot coals on their eyes than be seen carrying a basket of cosmetics into the communal shower area.

When our children leave home we must remember that, while we cannot stereotype our own sons and daughters, there is some truth to the fact that boys and girls (or men and women) deal with problems differently. We must keep this in mind while we watch them grow up and pull away from us. This hit home for me the first time I traveled with Stu and his cello.

By the time we starting looking for colleges, Stu was quite used to traveling with his cello in tow. He had taken it to Hawaii, Australia, and New Zealand. It was not until he started auditioning for colleges, however, that I had my first experience traveling with this delicate yet cumbersome instrument. Regrettably, I had let the insurance lapse, and when we went to Tulsa the cello was essentially unprotected. But the case was strong, and we were particular about attending to it in the oversize baggage security area to ensure it was wrapped well for its journey. As we left the case in the care of the baggage handlers, I expressed a nagging concern to Stu about the well-being of the instrument. He shrugged his shoulders and told me not to worry. After all, it had been around the world with him. He was sure it would withstand one more trip.

When we arrived in Tulsa, he sauntered off to the oversize-baggage conveyor belt while I waited nervously for our other bags. After some time had passed, the cello had not been delivered. Stu called on his cell phone — no sign of the cello. He would wait a little longer. Finally the cello rattled over the rim of the conveyor belt for the regular luggage where I was waiting, its familiar red fragile stickers lurching in and out of sight as the cello case somersaulted onto the belt doing a complete flip and came clanking around the corner to where I was standing. I signaled to Stu on his cell phone. He came running over, grabbed the case, and plopped it down on the floor right there in the middle of the baggage claim area, his hands anxiously ripping off the duct tape that was holding the aging case together.

> *"I thought you weren't worried about it?" I could not resist teasing him even though I was as worried as he now appeared to be.*
>
> *"I just said that. I was worried enough for both us, so there was no point in you worrying as well."*

All was well with the cello, but I realized my teenage son had been protective of me and had not wanted me to worry on his behalf.

While men like to handle their own problems, women want to talk about their problems and air out the issues. This can be especially hard on girls in the beginning of their college career while they are still making friends and do not feel close to anyone. Once a girl is settled in at school and has a special friend or a social group that she can confide in, it gets much easier for her. At this point the tables turn, and it can be a difficult time for boys. Boys feel like it will be exposing them as vulnerable if they talk over how lonely they feel or what a hard time they are having in class. Many boys in their freshman year of college have reported that they envy girls having the freedom and willingness to be able to talk to each other about what they are going through. Boys privately admit to being just as lonely, scared, and homesick as girls, but they rarely admit to it in public and usually do not tell their parents unless they have an especially close relationship with them.

In my own case, I remember my early weeks of college, one hundred miles away from home, I went through the period of feeling desolate and lonely and having no one to talk to. I was not housed on campus, but I shared a room in town with another girl. Our landlady rented rooms to the university, so I was not exposed to dorm life and did not have the camaraderie of others who were lucky enough to get housed in a residence hall. My roommate made friends quickly and was often out, leaving me alone. Before long, I had enough of my lonely college experience. I packed my bags and put myself on a train back home. I arrived unannounced for the weekend and defiantly informed my father that I had left the university.

My scheme failed, however, and my father personally drove me back to the university before the weekend was over to deal with my loneliness.

Here are some other ways in which females and males away at college differ, but of course, there are no hard and fast rules:

- Females are more likely to be victims of "date rape." They may succumb to the pressure of having sexual intercourse before they are ready because everyone else is doing it. Or they may be the victims of rape.

- Males are more likely to have guns or other weapons on campus, even though they are prohibited by residence hall rules.

- Females are more likely to use diet aids, such as diet pills, and fall victim to anorexia, bulimia, and other eating disorders in an attempt to control their weight.

- Males are less likely to clean their rooms, organize their belongings, or participate in keeping common areas clean, such as kitchens.

- Females are more likely to call you when they are sick. Males are more likely to figure out what to do for themselves, or ignore the problem until it either goes away or becomes a big problem.

- Males pack less than females. Females will obsess over details, such as how many towels to pack. A male may not even remember to pack towels.

- A male may report not missing home, even though he does. A female may report missing home to the point where you begin to regret sending her, but that may not mean she wants to give up and come home.

- A girl is more likely to take care of necessities promptly, like replacing the shampoo when it runs out, whereas a boy may use his soap on his hair for weeks before he is motivated to replace the shampoo.

- Your daughter may want to shop with you for supplies and will want to choose every item. Your son will be oblivious, too busy, and uninterested in most things. He will be all too happy for to you pick out the supplies he needs and pack them for him.

An interesting phenomenon that occurs in college has to do with the maturity level of young men versus young women. Girls tend to mature earlier than boys do, which means throughout high school, girls are doing better in class, behaving better, and handling their emotions with more maturity than most boys. At some point though, boys have to catch up. In college, boys who have been slow to mature begin to reach a level of maturity that equals that of girls. Girls, who have been used to doing better in class than their male counterparts, suddenly find they are faced with some serious academic competition.

Both boys and girls, free from the constraints of curfews and parental supervision, tend to party pretty hard in college.

Interestingly though, although technical and engineering majors are still male dominated, on the whole, the percentage of women in college continues to grow, so that the ratio of men to women is swinging in favor of the women. This presents challenges to most colleges that would prefer to preserve a balance between males and females.

Whether you are sending a male or a female off to college, keep in mind that from the moment they leave home, their personality is in a state of flux as they seek to discover who they are and how to handle things. Male or female, they will be subject to new stresses that they have never experienced before, and they will be learning to how to deal with a variety of new situations. Whether or not they let you into the problems they are having, you have to trust, listen sympathetically, and let them come up with their own solutions.

SECTION

3

The Parents' Experience

CHAPTER 14

Missing Your Child

When my three boys were teenagers and all at home, the house was always full of their brusque, deep voices and teasing, yelling, cajoling, and laughing. Boys are competitive, and from morning to night, mine would be fighting or wrestling with each other over one minor issue or another. Boys do not so much interact by talking as they do by teasing and fighting, so there was always plenty of noise. In the thick of raising them, my head ached from the stresses of running back and forth to extracurricular events, keeping up with work, striving to provide a healthy dinner, and staying on top of laundry and grocery shopping, I longed for calmer days. Quietly, secretly, I looked forward to them leaving for college.

But when it finally started to happen and my first son went off to college, I was unprepared for how much I was going to miss him. I had spent most of his senior year and last summer at home making preparations. You prepare for high school graduation; you prepare for college. You monitor the mail and make sure all the forms are completed and returned on time. You get photographs made. You shop for extra long twin sheets. You make travel arrangements and think about last minute visits to family and friends. In quiet moments, you worry whether he will make the adjustment to college life without incident and what he will do if he gets sick or runs into car problems. All of this leaves no time for self-contemplation. It never even occurred to me that my son's departure would leave a massive void in my life. After all, I still had two sons left in the house.

Then the time came for him to depart and the reality hit me that there was no turning back. That was it. He was off to college and embarking on the first precarious steps of his adulthood. Sudden panic set in as I began to think about the meaning of having my firstborn child go away to college.

When my second son graduated high school, the feelings of pride I experienced on his behalf were mixed with grief on my own account. I knew from experience how much I was going to miss him and that now I was moving from being the parent of three children to being the parent of one child and two adults.

The orchestra struck up the first notes of Pomp and Circumstance; the students began to file into the familiar strains of that majestic march; the crowd of parents, grandparents, alumni, and relatives stood up as one body; and there rose up into the height of the World Arena the most amazing, noisy harmony of clapping, cheering, and whistling. My son, proud, cocky, and defiantly triumphant after a long, hard struggle with senior level math, biology, and history, walked past me, his gown flowing out behind him and his cap perched precariously on his head, leaning slightly too much to one side as though it might fall off at any minute. For my first son, I had cried tears of joy and pride. For my second son, I cried tears of mourning. Mourning for the passing of the happy times I spent raising him, laughing with him, even fighting with him. Mourning for the passing of the times I yelled at him to get up in the morning and rolled my eyes at him when at bedtime he would suddenly remember an unfinished homework assignment. I cried in remembrance of the intellectual conversations I had with him when he would tell me about his history classes, his theory of knowledge classes, and of heated debates in English class.

I was no less proud of Stu than I had been of Ian, but this time, I knew too well that graduation is not just the day that your child finishes high school. It marks the transition of your child into young adulthood and it marks the beginning of him leaving home forever.

The final summer before college rushes by in a flurry of preparations, freshman orientation, and summer job hunting, and culminates in the big goodbye. Your child goes off into the big, wide world with eyes and heart open to the flavor of new experience, and you trundle home to an empty house, haunted with the echoes of shared laughter, slamming doors, big fights, special moments, and happy times together — now, it is oh so quiet.

When your children leave home, it is hard to describe the variety of ways in which your emotions affect you. The entire dynamic of life at home changes when one person leaves, and even though you are happy for them and anxious for news about their new, exciting life, you wish they were back home, and that things were as they used to be.

For the first few weeks, everywhere you go and everything you do reminds you of them. I would sit on the family room sofa and remember how Ian used to make himself a cup of tea every night before going to bed. He would always leave the sugar bowl on the table instead of putting it back, and I would always put it back in its place on the counter when I went up to bed. After he left for college, that sugar bowl sat on the table for four days.

When Stu was at home, he used to sit on the sofa in the basement, which you could see from the top of the basement stairs. He would sit back with his feet on the coffee table, his laptop snuggled up against his knees, and he would be doing his instant messaging and sending e-mails to his friends. When I would come home through the garage door into the family room, I had a direct line of sight down the basement stairs to the familiar site of Stu on the sofa with his computer. After he left for college, it took a long time for me to shake off the habit of poking my head down the stairs to say hi. A couple of times I said "Hi Stu" even though I knew he was not there, and the echo of those two tiny words hung in the stairwell for what seemed like hours.

Like myself, Barb had raised three sons. She stayed home from work until they were all off to college. When Charlie, her last son, went off, she felt the emptiness in the house.

"The hardest part was going to his room

and doing a thorough cleaning. The sock that he had searched for found behind the bed, the book he had almost finished reading — everything brought with it a small wave of anxiety. "

When your children leave home, you learn things about them that you never knew before. Ian loves tortilla chips with salsa. When he left, an open bag of tortilla chips sat in the cupboard on the top shelf. Normally, I bought at least one bag every week. I continued to buy a bag a week until three bags of tortilla chips sat in the cupboard. After the third bag, I realized no one was eating them. Those bags of tortilla chips sat there on the shelf every day from August until Ian came home for Thanksgiving. While he was home, he polished off a couple of them and went away again. The last bag sat there until he came home for Christmas.

Focus on the Positive

There are positives that begin to emerge as times passes. When Stu left, I only had one son left in the house. I noticed that the one-pound bricks of cheese I had been buying were sitting in the back of the fridge, encased in mold. Again, I had not realized that Stu was the only one in the family who was eating the cheese. He was putting it away by the pound, and I had not noticed that it was only him. This resulted in quite a savings on my cheese budget.

Food consumption is just the beginning. Your utility bills will also drop. With two of my sons gone, my electric, gas, and water bills were lower than I had ever known them.

Not only was I saving money on running the household, but my workload was also considerably reduced. Instead of the required two loads of laundry that I used to do nightly to keep up with the washing, I could get all my laundry done on Saturday morning. Instead of running the dishwasher every night and twice on weekends, I could get away with running it once every two or three days. Instead of cooking every night, I could cook one night and freeze the food for the rest of the week or the weeks to come, so I did not have to scramble to find fast food at the last minute. I cooked less and ate better, not to mention much more cheaply.

Of course, all this meant I had more time to myself. More time, that is, that I had to fill up. And it did get lonely in the beginning, before I found more ways to use my time productively.

You cannot go on pining after your children. Eventually you will start to reclaim your own life. Barb is a single mom who had been devoted to raising her children and stayed home until the last one was off on his own. She found that even though she missed her son, she did enjoy having time to herself:

> *"It surprised me how much I enjoy time alone in the house. It's peaceful and relaxing with very few interruptions. I'm entirely on my own schedule and the weekends are wonderful. I'm even*

considering dating again, which I would never do as long as I was raising children."

If you are married, this is a good time to rekindle your relationship with your spouse. After years of using the "divide and conquer" routine, you doing the grocery shopping perhaps, while your spouse ran the after-school activity taxi service, this is a good time to look for something you can do together, whether it is finding an activity, attending sporting events, or taking a cruise. Spend some time together and rediscover who you have each become over the course of the child-raising years.

If you have other children at home, it is a nice opportunity for the rest of your children to benefit from a little more focused attention. Our oldest children get all of our attention until a sibling comes along. The younger siblings have never known what it is to enjoy the undivided attention of a parent. This time can be of great benefit to them, especially if they are teenagers and well on their road to independence. This is a great time in their life to give them a little extra attention.

CHAPTER 15

Parenting a College Student

Parenting a college student is a different level of parenting than we have previously experienced. We are no longer parenting children, and as our children traverse the college years, we are no longer parenting teenagers. We have moved up into the big leagues of parenting — parenting young adults. So much is going on in our lives and our children's lives when we send them off to college that sometimes it is hard to remember they no longer need to be treated as children.

During the teenage years and high school, we watch our children wrestle with becoming adults. They are confidently talking down to us one minute and experiencing an emotional breakdown the next for reasons that sometimes seem trivial to us. We watch them flip-flop back and forth between doing things their way and asking us for help. Sometimes we give them more help than they want and they think we are nagging them, and other times we give them a lot of elbow-room and then wonder if we should have kept a tighter control over a situation that goes awry.

But while we sometimes are not sure how much to interfere while they are in high school, when our children get to college it is almost never right to interfere. The only two exceptions to this are:

- If your student expressly requests your help.

- If you suspect or know for a fact that something is amiss.

For all situations that fall into the non-life-threatening category, we should endeavor, if called on, to help our student resolve the issues successfully by themselves by helping them sort through ideas and solutions of their own, rather than rushing in and proactively fixing things.

If not called on, it is best to keep out of it altogether, unless you sense there is a serious, potentially life-threatening situation at hand.

I have been puzzled, as my children have gone off to college, how much the college itself keeps parents involved in their children's lives with their constant deluge of literature and information. They offer a parent weekend so you can come and check in on your student, they inundate you with literature about the alumni association and the parent association, and they send you flyers and solicitations to send gift baskets for exam week. Some even solicit parent recommendations for teacher awards — as if our students talk to us in detail about their teachers and how they are doing in class!

While I appreciate information from the college and I like getting plenty of information about my children, it seems it makes it harder to remember that this is a time to let go and not hold on to our children. We know deep down inside this is a transition time for our children to grow up and deal with their own problems, and college is really their thing, not ours (if you discount the paying for it part, which most students are happy to leave squarely in their parents' court). It is best to let them try to figure things out, sort out their own issues, decide on their own class schedules, choose their own major, and so on.

It is the real test of our parenting to date. Because the truth is, how they will behave over the course of the next few years is not so much influenced by which college they decide to attend or whether they decide to join a fraternity. Instead, it will be guided by how we, as their parents, raised them since they were born — what beliefs, morals, and codes of conduct we have guided them to adopt or role-modeled for them in our own behavior. In fact, if we have been close to our children, then in times of crisis they are likely to respond exactly how we would or at least how we would have responded at their age.

Changing Beliefs

You may notice, as you see your student between semester breaks, that they are experimenting with belief systems and value systems that are not your own. This is not necessarily a cause for concern. Now that they are free to break away from us, it is natural that they will go through a period of experimentation, trying on different opinions and beliefs until they are ready to decide what their adult character is going to be. Most normal students, even as they experiment with changing opinions, will revert to the standards by which they were raised when a crisis presses them to a knee-jerk reaction. In other words, despite the outward impression of a personality in flux, their core belief system, which they still hold onto below the surface, is essentially unchanged from whatever it was. Most students tend to do the right thing in a crisis.

Appearance

Along with their changing belief system, you may notice changes in appearance. Sometimes these may be subtle and other times they may hit you in the face. Perhaps your student arrives home sporting several new body piercings or tattoos. One conservative friend of mine was proud that his son made it into Colorado School of Mines, a prestigious engineering school where the ratio of boys to girls is about 3:1. He felt for sure his son was on a sound academic track in a school that was not renowned for social antics.

His tall, dark, and handsome son arrived home after his first semester away at college, wearing a baseball cap, which he seemed rather reluctant to remove. After further exploration, Steve, the boy's father, was shocked to discover that his son had died his hair platinum blonde. Steve, a computer science engineer, was of course upset. He screamed and yelled at his son and told him how much he was embarrassed to be seen with him. But the boy was only reacting to his new freedom after years of being subject to Steve's tyrannical rule.

A little experimentation with one's adulthood is perfectly

natural and should be tolerated with patience as our children go through the process of discovering who they are, what there beliefs are, what they like, and how they want to look.

Communication

Despite the fact that children today have access to a wide variety of communication tools, why is that we still do not hear from them as often as we would sometimes like? These days, the average student has easy access to instant messaging, texting, phone, and e-mail. We puzzle over the fact that Junior spent every waking moment he was not in school sitting at the computer in the family room instant messaging with his friends. Yet when we send him a simple text message, days go by and we do not hear back.

Relax, there is nothing wrong. They are just busy having their own life, and they do not feel the need to report back to us every minute. As anxious parents sitting at home biting our nails, it is hard for us to remember that most students, after the first few weeks of college, have an active life both academically and socially, and they are absorbed in it.

It helps to remember that as adults we each have our preferred methods of communication. Some of us prefer to e-mail, while others prefer to call on the phone. Your children are the same, and when trying to reach them to see how they are doing, it will help to use the method your children prefer.

Joy and her daughter, Heather, are close and were always in touch by cell phone when Heather lived at home. When Heather left for college, Joy missed talking to her. Now that Heather is in college, Joy finds that e-mail works best to communicate with her.

> *"We stay in touch via e-mail, text messaging, and phone calls. She usually doesn't call unless something is wrong, so I tend to panic when I see her on the caller ID."*

Barb is sensitive to the fact that her son's college schedule is different from when he lived at home:

> *"I use e-mail more than he does, but he will use the phone more than I will. I don't like to call him, because I don't want to interrupt a class, studying, or his sleeping late after a long night of studying. I wait until he calls me."*

Remember that everyone is different. One of my sons calls every week. He likes to hear what is going on at home. I find this interesting since he hates the telephone, and when all the boys were at home he would always be the last one to pick up the phone if it rang.

My other son in college is completely the opposite. If the phone rang at home, he was right there. A ringing phone was like a magnet to him and, no matter who was at home to answer it, he usually had the phone answered by the second ring. This same son spent all his free time, night and day, instant messaging and doing his e-mail. But I rarely hear from him. Sometimes I will drop him an e-mail and ask him to call me. I just want to know he is alive and safe. Sometimes I notice that Chris, my youngest son who lives at home, is talking to his brother on his cell phone. This at least lets me know that Stu is alive and doing all right and I do not worry about him. I know he will call me when he needs my help with something. This is usually about a week before the semester gets out. He calls to find out what arrangements I have made to get him home! Sometimes I send him an e-mail and ask him to call me. This is better than me calling him because no matter what time I choose to call, he will answer the phone, and halfway through my first sentence he will tell me that he is in a hurry and needs to be somewhere. So when I wait until he calls me I know he has time to talk. I try to keep my conversations short unless he is in the mood to talk.

Eating Their Vegetables

I believe that whether your student is eating salad with dinner in the dining hall, living on pizza and beer, or getting into serious drug abuse at frat parties has a lot to do with what they learned growing up and what kind of personality they have. Not all, but many, students are drinking on campus. That is a fact. Some are doing drugs. Let us face it — most of our children had easy access to drugs in high school. They are in even more plentiful supply on college campuses. But that does not mean every student is using.

Whether your children are using drugs or not is probably related to what they have learned so far in life and how they deal with resisting peer pressure.

We cannot shelter our children from life. The thing to note is that by the time our children are high school seniors, it is already too late to have much influence over how they will turn out. The time to begin is early in their childhood. It always bothers me when parents try to shelter their children from life itself. If there are drugs in the high school, it is better to talk to our children about it before they get to high school and give them some tools to deal with it, rather than hunt high and low for the elusive high school environment that is truly drug free.

I did not go to a big city high school. It was a relatively conservative school in the suburbs. Nonetheless, there were drugs in my high school several decades ago. It is a real problem, but we must teach our children to deal with it. If we have done a good job, they will not get into too much trouble once they get out on their own because they will know which choices to make.

As for eating vegetables, the first thing to remember is that your student probably will not die or suffer malnutrition if they skip vegetables for a while. The second thing to note is that if their diet at home provided them easy access to a variety of fruits and vegetables, some of which they ate and some of which they did not, they are likely to do the same thing in college. If you pressured them to sit at the table and not get up until they ate their vegetables, then of course the first thing they will do when out on their own is enjoy the pure pleasure of eating, or not eating, whatever they like.

Going to Church

Studies show that the majority of college students do not attend church, even if they were raised to go every Sunday as children. Even though I raised my sons to go to church on Sundays, I am not surprised by the fact they do not attend church while in college. When they come home, I give them the option of whether to attend with me. While they were under 18, church was not optional. I do not believe church-going (and not going) has much to do with attending college. When we are children, religion is either thrust upon us or it is left out. When we grow up, it is normal to go through a period of exploration to determine our belief system. Church is typically not a choice when we are young. Either our family goes or does not go. As we grow, we need to learn now to make our own choices. Many young adults who leave the church tend to come back when they are older or when they have children of their own.

Religion is personal. Even if your religion is important to you, you cannot make this choice for your children after they have grown. We all need to make our own choices. Your children are more likely to come back by themselves if left alone than if constantly nagged about it by their overzealous parents. So be careful when talking about this topic with your student.

It goes both ways. My friend Janet was surprised that

her son developed quite an interest in religion. Her son, Shane, became very involved with Campus Crusade for Christ. He even raised money to spend his college vacations doing projects for them. He led Bible studies on campus as well as at the Denver Detention Center.

If you are a church-going person yourself, you may find it easier to support your student's decision to attend church rather than his decision to not attend church. But it does not pay to pressure him or to stress over it. Pressuring him is likely to have the reverse effect and stressing over it is not good for your health. Try having a wait-and-see attitude and being patient as your child finds his own way in life.

Waking Up

Since you have lived with your teenagers for several years prior to their departure for college, you have no doubt realized that they do not live on the same schedule as the rest of us.

Our schedules are driven by our working hours. The need to get up early and get off to work for 20, 30, or 40 years has set our body clocks on a schedule that we adhere to most of the time, even when we do not need to go to work.

College students do not need to live in the same paradigm as working adults. They are free to create their class schedules to suit their preferred waking and sleeping habits.

Colleges acknowledge this. After visiting multiple college campuses, I noticed that most colleges do not open the dining hall for breakfast on the weekends. I concluded that sleeping until one in the afternoon on weekends must not be a habit that is observed exclusively by my own children. It must be a widespread phenomenon. Indeed, if I think back to my own college years, I was the same.

If your students have several early classes, you may be worried that they will not get up in time. Do not worry. There may be times when they do not get up in time and you will probably never know about it. Somehow your student will survive the class and may even pass it. In fact, most do.

When they need to get up, they will. When Stu came home for his first Thanksgiving break, he had been gone from home over four months without seeing any of his family or friends. He was absolutely dying to come home for Thanksgiving. I booked him a flight that departed at one in the afternoon. I figured that would give him plenty of time to wake up and make the journey to the airport. Then, at the last minute, the flight was moved up by two hours. After calculating the new time, that he would need to get through security on a busy Thanksgiving holiday, his travel time to the airport, and the time he would need to wake up and get ready to leave, we figured out that he would have to get up at 7:00 a.m. — I was worried. Stu's record for waking himself up early was not stellar.

The night before the flight, we spoke on the phone. I

urged him to take additional precautions for waking up on time and not missing his flight:

> *"Remember that extra alarm clock I bought you when your luggage didn't arrive? Why don't you set them both. That way if you miss waking up to one you will wake up to the other."*

> *"Don't worry, Mom. Remember I told you that I bought some speakers for my laptop; well when I have to get up for my early classes I route my iPod alarm clock through the speakers and it really booms. I'll get up in time."*

He called from the airport to let me know he was on time for the plane. He explained that he awoke before any of his alarms went off.

> *"What really woke me was my friend tapping gently on the door and asking if I wanted to travel to the airport with him."*

Stu was so eager to get home that a gentle tap on the door woke him even though he needed thundering alarms to wake him up for math class.

They will get up when it is important (to them, anyway). So do not worry about them.

Dealing with Their Problems

I developed my philosophy to dealing with my children's problems while they were in middle school. As children grow into teenagers, it becomes more and more embarrassing for them to have their parents step in and sort things out. They would tell me their stories, as all children do, of unfair treatment in class; how a teacher gave them a bad grade for a missed assignment and let another child make the assignment up and get an A; or how a child trod on their calculator, stole their scissors, or ripped a page in one of their textbooks.

I would always offer to step in and speak to a teacher, call the principal, or call another child's mother. Without exception, the answer from all three of my children was always the same.

"No. It's okay. I'll manage."

Teenagers would rather put up with all kinds of unfair conditions, cruelties, and teasing by their peers than have a parent go marching up to the school to "sort things out."

When they get to college, they are trying even more to be grown-up and independent. Unless your student has a reason to request your help, it is better not to step in. Try to refrain from calling the Dean of the college or the residence hall staff to see if your child is alright. The first thing they are going to do is come and get your student. There is no way to make an anonymous phone call to the school to find out if your child is alright.

Just because your student calls to complain on the phone about how bad things are does not mean they are requesting help. And it can be quite funny to them in retrospect, after they solve the problem and look back on the situation. My friend Tom tells this story about his son's first year in college:

> *"My oldest son was living with a roommate for the first time. One night he called upset and totally frustrated. When I asked what was wrong, he told me he was fed up with his roommate. His long-time friend was sloppy, messy, and not doing his chores. I had to laugh as my son was learning what I was unable to teach at home — that cleaning and chores were important! I still laugh with him about this phone call."*

Most of the time they will solve their own problems and will not need our interference, only our support.

Identifying a Real Problem

It can be difficult to tell if your student is experiencing a real problem of a serious nature that calls for parental interference. They probably will not tell you. It will probably build up slowly at first, and then escalate when the situation is already serious by the time you find out about it. If this is the case, keep in mind that your student probably took time trying to solve the problem alone, so do not get too angry about the fact that he did not tell you right away. Just move in swiftly and try to help him solve it. If you make a big fuss, he will hesitate even longer before coming to you next time.

If you receive any personal communication from the college about your student, see it as a red flag and act immediately. Colleges rarely communicate directly with parents, so if they do you should treat it as a definitive call to action.

Pay attention to little things that your student may tell you and follow up on little things (in a subtle way if possible) next time you communicate. Things like whether they are enjoying social interaction, how they are doing in class, and whether they are in good health are difficult things to talk about with our children without sounding like we are prying or interfering in their right to privacy and independence. But these all hold clues as to their well-being.

Sarah, of UniversityParent, tells us that missing class and poor academic performance are signs to watch for. She goes on to say:

> *"Students tend to be most successful when they find a group on campus, such as an academic program, intramural team, and Greek house — just some way they can be involved and find peer role models. It makes big campuses feel manageable."*

It could be as simple as joining a club or having a regular group of friends in the residence hall, but as soon as students settle in with friends and develop a routine of sorts, they tend to do better.

Avoid Nagging

When our children are small and they first experiment with crayons, we praise them for their art as though they were the next Picasso. We do this even if their man looks like a green one-eyed monster and their dog looks more like a fish. Somewhere between childhood and adulthood, if we are not careful, our praise has a tendency to turn to criticism and nagging. When your student calls to tell you they have resolved a problem by themselves, remind yourself how you praised them for their art and remember they are still becoming adults and still experimenting with their own maturity. Do not focus on the actual solution they came up with any more than you did on that one-eyed, green monster — just praise them for solving the problem. The better the support they get from home, the more they will build confidence.

Growing Old Gracefully

Our children may never solve problems the same way we would. They are from a different generation with a different perspective on life. But rest assured that they will get better at it as they go on, and trust that they will eventually become competent and worthy adults.

Carol Barkin graduated from Harvard University. Having lived through the experience of sending her son to college, she went on to write the book *When Your Kid Goes to College: A Parent's Survival Guide*. She makes an astute observation about our own self perceptions when our children grow up and start making their own decisions and solving their own problems:

> *"It can be a difficult realization for parents, who sometimes try to hold on to the control and the responsibilities longer than they should. Having a child who's an adult means you're older than you might wish or secretly pretend to yourself; you've moved into a different generation, and you may not like the idea."*

Facing the fact that we are aging may be the hardest part of watching our children grow up. Once we are ready to face the fact that we are on the cusp of moving out of our prime and into our golden years, we are able to sit back and enjoy the experience of watching our children move into life's spotlight as the generation that is driving business, driving industry, driving the new direction of society, and taking the world forward into the next great era. This is a much easier and more comfortable perspective than trying to hang on to control over their career decisions, their spending habits, and the social hours they keep with their friends.

Accepting your age with grace does not mean you have to sit back in your rocking chair and start knitting shawls. Rather, it allows to you accept that it is alright to slow down. It can be peaceful not having to worry about your children. You have done your part, and while you will always be a mother or a father to your children, it is not necessary to parent them constantly once they have moved away.

CHAPTER 16

The New Family Dynamic

When your sons or daughters left for college for the first time, they were nervous and scared (even if they did not admit it). By the time they make their first trip home, whether only a week or two into the semester or not until Thanksgiving or even Christmas break, they have a sense of adulthood and being able to cope by themselves that they did not have before.

While they were gone, you and any remaining members of your family have settled into a new routine and a new dynamic.

Both you and your student are expecting that when they come back home things will somehow be just what they were before they left. This is rarely the case.

Coming Home

While they lived with you, your children had to live by your rules. Now that they have spent time away, your rules make little sense to them. For one thing, even relatively conservative students have probably developed a habit of going to bed later than they did at home. It no longer makes sense to wait up and worry over the whereabouts of a student who has roamed across campus at two in the morning from a late-night feeding frenzy at the local hot wings house several hundred miles from home.

This has pluses and minuses. When Ian took a summer job at a pizza restaurant during his first summer after freshman year, I no longer felt obligated to stay up and wait for him to come home, since it was often after one a.m. and I had a full-time job to get up and go to. However, if I woke up in the night to go to the bathroom, I would still sneak a peek out the front window to check if his car was in the driveway. You cannot stop being a parent.

When I met Stu at the airport to bring him home for Christmas break, one of his first questions to me was how I was going to treat him. He wanted to know if he would have a curfew now that he had lived out on his own. I explained to him that while I was not going to hold him to an 11 p.m. curfew, I still expected him to tell me, out of common courtesy, when he expected to be home. I told him this was not an effort to control him, merely the means by which I would sleep soundly and not worry about him. You cannot expect to get up and go missing for long periods of time right under your mother's nose and not expect her to worry. That is just how it works for mothers. He seemed to buy that explanation and was consequently respectful about making sure I knew where he was and when he was expecting to come home.

For my part, as long as I had some idea where he was, I tried not to give him the third degree and always asked him if he had a good time when he came back to the house.

Home Is a Hotel Syndrome

If you have already experienced one child leaving home, you may relate to this scenario. Your daughter is due home from college. You have not seen her in three months. You ache for her, for times to be as they were a year ago. You have so much to tell her. You want to show her the new carpet you put in your bedroom and show off the changes you have made in the living room. You want to hear all about college, how she is doing, what her social life is like, and what she misses from home. You cannot wait to pick her up at the airport, bus station, or wherever.

At last, you both arrive home. She opens the fridge, grabs a soda, goes down into the basement with her cell phone glued to her ear, fires up the computer, and instant messages her friends for the next two hours. You have shopped, you have planned, and her favorite dinner is on the menu tonight. As you are about to start preparing her favorite meal as though it were her last, she announces that she will not be home for dinner. After all, she is only going to be at home for a few days and she simply must go and see her best friends from high school. After a frustrating evening home alone, by midnight you wonder whether you should go to bed or stay up longer and worry.

This is not like when the children were little and you planned a family Christmas. It is natural that students want to continue exercising their newfound freedom when they come home. Once you make progress in life, you cannot go back (nor would you want to). It is natural as well that they will want to visit with their old friends and swap college stories with their high school peers. Who else will better understand what they are going through? Or relate to their funny stories about their roommate? By interacting with their peers, they will get new ideas on how to cope, and get a feeling that their problems are common and they are not alone.

Unless they are taking advantage of you or behaving in truly inappropriate ways, it is better to just let them grow up. You can feel secure in the knowledge that they feel enough at home to dump the laundry and run off with their friends. You do not want them to be clingy, stay-at-homes types with no friends to visit or interests of their own to pursue.

Do Not Make Plans for Your Student

When your son or daughter returns home from school, whether for a flying visit at Thanksgiving or for three months in the summer, it will be less frustrating all around if you do not make plans for your them. It was one thing when they were 10-years-old, and you told them they had to spend Sunday afternoon at grandma's house. Now that they are older and have found their own independence, expect them to have plans of their own. If you wish to go visit your mother on Sunday afternoon, there is no reason why you should stop or change your plans. Carry on as if your student were not at home. This is the easiest way to avoid frustrating confrontations. Ten minutes or so before you are due to leave, casually mention to your son or daughter that you are off to visit so-and-so and invite them to come along. If they have nothing else going on, and they have been hanging around the house all day, they are more likely to come along just for something to do. If you plan two weeks ahead and constantly remind them to keep Sunday afternoon free, they will feel like you are cramping their style and nagging them to do things they do not want to do.

No Expectations

One parent confessed to feeling let down when she went to pick her student up for Thanksgiving. After making a 10-hour car journey and an overnight stay in a hotel, she was looking forward to the ride home with her daughter who she had not seen for three months. She pictured herself with her daughter catching up on all kinds of news, making the ride back home seem like half the journey.

Instead, her daughter got in the car, spent five minutes telling her mother how tired she was after her final exams, and then put her earphones on and spent eight of the next 10 hours sleeping. She woke up to eat, take a bathroom break, and ask her mother how much farther they had to go.

Students get tired at college. They have so many more

things to think about than when they were at home. They do their own laundry, stay up all kinds of hours at night, study hard for exams, and take care of all their own personal needs. Well, you may say, so do you, and what is more, you have to mow the lawn, repair the fence, maintain a full-time job outside the home, and cook and clean for a family of four. But you have many years experience doing this, and your student does not.

Staying out at night, partying, and cramming all night for exams is part of college life. It is what happens. Accepting that students will come home tired and in need of rest, and then run off and conduct their own life with their friends will make life at home much easier on you. Your relaxed attitude, in turn, will foster an environment in which your students feel safe to grow up and exert their independence, not just at college, but also at home. Is it not better that you should give them the freedom, rather than have them conduct a life of mystery behind your back?

A friend of my son's graduated from high school and went off to St. Louis to attend college, leaving behind her boyfriend, whom her parents disapproved of. My son's friend, let us call her Jane, missed her boyfriend, but her parents would not authorize a trip home. So instead, Jane snuck home behind her parents back. We are not sure how she was found out; her parents were livid. Not only did she take the long car trip alone, without giving them the opportunity to "watch out for her," but also she deprived them of the chance to visit with them while she was home. If her parents had been willing to let her make the trip home in the first place, a lot of heartache, anger, and resentment would have been avoided.

It Goes Both Ways

I am still not sure whether I feel proud or guilty about the following incident. I offer it as an example of how children, too, are affected by the change in the family dynamic. When they left, they were the center of attention. Upon their return, they can sometimes feel that there is not as much room for them as there once was. Even though they want to grow up and move away from home, it can still be a shock for them to discover that your life has moved on without them.

My son was in his second year of college. He drove his car out there at the beginning of the year. It is almost 600 miles from Colorado Springs to Lincoln, Nebraska. At Thanksgiving he was very excited.

"This is actually the longest I have been away from home by myself," he told me on the phone. In his first year, he had to make frequent trips home to keep up with his orthodontic treatment. (Side note: if you think your children will go away to college, do not wait until junior year to get their braces! If the treatment drags on for any reason, you will have to arrange frequent trips home when they start college.) Ian was looking forward to driving himself home for Thanksgiving, and he was only half an hour out of Lincoln when my phone rang. I happened to be on the way to an important first business meeting for a new venture I was trying to get off the ground. This

was not just any business meeting, but the start of a new career and a new life for me.

Something was wrong with Ian's car. It had slowed down and died to a halt, with steam cascading out from under the hood.

> *"I think it must have overheated or something."*

> *"Have you called Dad?"*

> *"I can't reach Dad. I called AAA and I can't reach them either. You are the only one I have been able to reach."*

This was a bad time for me to be taking an emergency call that demanded my full attention. I simply could not be late for my meeting.

> *"I have to get to this meeting, and I'm already running late. Let me get there and explain to them that I have to deal with an emergency. Then I will call you back." And I hung up on him. My poor son was stranded by the side of the road, eager to get home for Thanksgiving and unable to make contact with anyone else. But I had my new life and it had to go on!*

I had equipped him with a cell phone, a car charger for the cell phone, a credit card, and a membership in the American Automobile Association. He was supposedly equipped to cope. And indeed he did cope, admirably in the end. But I recognized I was at a turning point as his parent, and he knew he needed to step up and get on with things. I did sneak in a quick call to his father before I went into my meeting, leaving him to his own devices.

It was an amazingly proud moment when I met him at the Greyhound bus station in Colorado Springs. He had managed to survive what to me had been the worst possible scenario. The car breaking down on a lonely road in Nebraska in the dead of winter at Thanksgiving break — a break so short that there was not much slack time to get over hurdles like loss of transport. He had taken care of the problem, found the right solution, and found his way home.

I was also proud of myself. As he stepped off the bus with temperatures in the twenties after a major crisis, and a lot of waiting around in the cold wearing nothing but denim shorts, a T-shirt, and a light jacket, I did not say a word about the way he was dressed. I simply hugged him and welcomed him home.

It does not take a major incident for your young adult to sense that things are changing, not just with them, but also with you. It is not unusual for a student, each time he comes home, to feel like a little more of a stranger, or a visitor to your home instead of coming back to their own house. Students notice that little things are different — a new sofa, a new car, a new kitchen counter, or new carpet. Slowly, one by one, things are changing in your house and old familiar things are being replaced with things they do not recognize and do not identify with. When they are gone for three months at a time and return home only for a few days, it is hard for them absorb the changes into their feeling of home and gradually they sense that this is no longer their place, their hangout, their identity. It is yours.

Each time they return to their own life, friends, and things at college, it feels a little more like their home to them, more familiar, more their own. Each time they come home, it feels a little less like their home, and a lot more like just their parent's house.

I remember feeling this poignantly myself. My parents were tea addicts and the electric kettle was always on the boil in preparation for the ritual cup of tea. It was white with a silver lid. No matter where my parents went, no matter how long they were gone, from minutes to days, the first thing they always did when they walked in the door was put the kettle on. My parents making tea in that old familiar white tea kettle was symbolic to me of being home.

One day I came home from college and the kettle was gone. It had been replaced by a tall blue kettle that was completely unfamiliar to me. Inside something jarred, and I knew this was not my home any more. It was my parents' home, and they had the right to buy a new tea kettle if they felt like it. But even though I did not drink tea, I missed the old white kettle.

Siblings at Home

With two of his brothers now in college, Chris, my youngest son, opened the refrigerator door at the end of his first week as an only child. He took a step back in fake amazement:

> *"Oh my God, there's still soda in the fridge. This rocks!"*

Over the next few weeks he dramatically remarked on how cool it was to get the computer whenever he wanted it, how he could leave his candy or his money lying around and no one would take it, and how he always got to sit in the front seat of the car. He reveled in the newfound attention that was being lavished on him by both parents. I always had time and energy to help with his homework, run out for last minute school supplies, pick him up from early release days, and so on.

However, after a few weeks he began to show signs of loneliness. He started talking about missing his brothers. There was never anyone to ask about his math homework. He missed having someone to talk to about his teachers. As the youngest of three, there were always at least two others who had trod the path before him, showing him the way, and to give him brotherly advice. There was no one to show him the way anymore. He realized that in exchange for more soda than he could ever drink, there was a void where his brothers had once been.

Parents of more than one child will notice a tendency in themselves, especially if their children are close in age, to push the oldest one faster into adulthood, and try to hold the youngest one back as long as possible. Now more than ever there is a danger that once the first sibling has flown the nest, we are more likely to treat the remaining child or children with more attention. We have more time and attention to spare on our youngest than we ever have before. This creates an environment where we can subconsciously hold the youngest back. The oldest was forced to find independence early because we did not have time or energy to spend. Now we are liable to prevent the youngest from growing up. At the least, we risk spoiling them in ways the oldest never got to experience.

If you have more than one child, you will notice a substantial shift in the dynamic between siblings as well. In the beginning, the older, returning child will lord it over the younger one and brag about their independence, accusing their younger sibling of knowing nothing, and of having no experience. College students will tell their high school brothers and sisters that they have no idea what life is about — as though they know it all now, after three short months away from home. But this is just your oldest child stretching his wings and learning to gather his self confidence. Truth is, they are just on the edge of learning what it is they do not know about life, but the last strains of teenage-hood still have their hold. While they have glimpsed their own vulnerability in the big wide world, they are not quite ready to admit it. So they come home and taunt younger siblings.

If you have more than two children, when the first one leaves the nest, the younger ones may develop a tighter bond. Many people with three or more children remark that the bond tightens between those left at home, and the number of fights in the house among siblings decreases. This can cause tension when the oldest returns. He or she senses the bond is stronger than before and feels left out. The same effect can occur if you only have two children, but the bond tightens between the parent and sibling left at home. The oldest, returning child senses this closeness and can become irritable at feeling left out in his own home, where he once dominated.

The fact is that if you have two children, they either become close growing up or develop some sort of tolerance for living with each other. Once one of them moves away the pattern is broken. This can cause a disturbance when the child that left returns, changed by their growing up experience. There is a sense of loss on all sides. Things can never be the same again.

It may help to remember that the first one or two visits are the worst. After that a sort of adaptation takes place. By the third or fourth visit, your young adult is developing a new self-confidence and has developed a sense of what to expect upon returning home. He no longer expects things to be as they were, but realizes the dynamic has changed and has adapted. The same thing happens with you and with other siblings. After a few visits, you begin to adjust to the new family dynamic. It is the first visit or two that are the hardest.

One friend used to dread coming back home to the house while her two daughters both lived there. She would return to a cacophony of yelling and fighting that ensued whenever the girls were left alone. However, when her oldest daughter returned home after her first semester away at college, things changed dramatically. My friend reported that she was amazed one day when she came home from a shopping trip and was greeted by the sound of laughter. Her two girls, having not seen each other for several months, were catching up, "talking about boys and makeup," and laughing together like every mother dreams her daughters should.

You may find that the college years are truly the best time in parenting. Your children are still living under the same roof, so you are able to witness first hand what you have longed for all your life: peace in the home. You hear the joyous sounds of laughter; your offspring getting along together and playing happily; talking about boys and makeup, or girls and football; or discussing life's deeper meaning. However they manifest, enjoy these moments if you are lucky enough to be witness to them. The time is coming when your children will move away and these moments will no longer be possible. These fleeting moments of life pick us up and make us feel good to be alive. And yes, you should congratulate yourself. You did a good job if you brought your children to this point.

CHAPTER 17

The Transition into Adulthood

Knowing when to step in and help or how far to let out the reins is one of the most puzzling aspects of parenthood. One of my earliest realizations about parenthood came when my first son was only a day or two old. I had envisioned having this baby doll that would eat when I was ready to feed him and sleep when I laid him down in his crib. The reality was quite different. He wanted to eat when I wanted to sleep, would not sleep when I wanted to eat, and always slept when I wanted to show him off to my friends and family. He had his own mind and as a newborn, he was already using it.

As our children grow, we waiver back and forth between controlling them closely and giving them free reign until they hurt themselves, trying to find the right balance. Sending them off to college can be our ultimate test of parenthood. Should we call them if they do not call us? Should we worry if we have not heard from them in days? Does a brief text message count as communication, or should we expect them to call and talk for an hour at least once a week? If we know they are having trouble with something, should we step in and offer them advice? Most colleges offer parents plenty of information and hotlines, but is it ever right to call them and ask them to check up on our students for us? These questions keep us up at night while our students are out nonchalantly eating pizza in the all-night fast food place across the street from the residence hall at three in the morning with their new friends.

Develop a Life of Your Own

As your son or daughter matures into adulthood they begin to see their parents, perhaps for the first time in their lives, as adults in their own right, not just as parents. Even though your children are pulling away from you, role modeling for them is just as important as ever because they begin to see you with new eyes. This is a good time to develop your own life, to do that volunteer work you have always thought about, to make a career move in a new direction, or simply to join a club to make new friends.

Of course, it is not for your children you are doing this, even though it will be good example for them, but rather for you. Shifting the focus in your life at this stage from them to you is a healthy move. You have spent the last 18 years caring for and worrying about this child, and it is hard to break the habit. Developing a new focus for your own life will help you break the habit of constantly focusing on your child.

As your child begins to see you in a new light, you begin to see yourself in a new light. It all fits together. When your life is full of interesting new activity you will find it easier to treat your child as another adult, instead of as a child, because he is no longer the center of the universe. Your child, in turn, will start to behave like an adult because you are treating him like one. But it takes a while to get there. In the meantime, for at least a year or two after they enter college, you are still the parent of a teenager.

The Teenage Sloth

The first summer vacation back at home starts out on a high note. You welcome home your estranged sons or daughters with joy and excitement. You have made their bed, dusted their room, gone grocery shopping for all their favorite foods, and done everything else you can think of to welcome them home.

For the first day or two you have lots to talk about and you enjoy hearing all the antics about what other college students do to disappoint their parents, how they skip classes, overdraft their bank account, go on drinking binges, and pull down a D in math.

Then the first couple of weeks of summer go by and junior still has not gotten himself a summer job. You are still patient and you give him a few odd jobs around the house to fill in the time while you are at work and he is waiting for the phone to ring with a job offer.

Then a couple more weeks go by. You come home from work tired and worn, to find Junior stretched out across the sofa, his expensive laptop precariously teetering on his lap looking likely to crash to the floor any second, his tousled head thrown back in peaceful slumber, his eyes tightly closed, and gentle snoring sounds emitting from his mouth and nose.

After you deftly catch the laptop, just as it begins to topple downward, you make your weary way into the kitchen. The kitchen counter is covered with dirty plates and cups that have been there since morning, and the family room is strewn with empty soda cans, and an assortment of packets of various types of junk food. All left half opened and happily abandoned. As you begin to pick up the empties you realize the garbage can is overflowing and has been pressed down so many times to avoid emptying it that the liner is stretched to the point of breaking and is now so overloaded that it will not come out.

You finally get the liner out of the garbage can and start to pick your way to the garage, but it is now dripping something gooey from the hole made by the compacted soda cans. You swing the garbage bag to the left because the expensive jacket you gave to your high school graduate so he may be properly clothed to go out into the big wide world, is now casually draped on the floor right in front of the door to the garage and you do not want to drip goo on it. Besides, it already sports a couple of muddy size 11 footprints.

Rustled by the noise of the garage door opener, Junior, who has apparently spent the entire day sleeping and eating, lifts his dreamy head, opens his eyes and mumbles, *"What's for dinner?"*

If this is not the experience with you have with your new

college student, you should count yourself among the lucky ones.

Summer Ultimatums

It makes things hard all around when after several months of relative freedom in college, a student is suddenly called back to order by frustrated parents and subjected to new restrictions or ultimatums. But the tough love approach is often the only remediation tactic left for a student out of control and a parent who is feeling taken advantage of.

I remember a friend of mine telling me about the ultimatum that she issued to her daughter upon finding her house continuously trashed every day for an entire summer.

My friend, let us call her Anne, was at her wit's end when her daughter, let us call her Kayla, finished her sophomore year. She was not doing well in college, having received only Cs and Ds that year. Anne suspected that she lived in a social whirlwind of partying and drinking. When Kayla came home that summer, she had gained 20 pounds, been kicked off the volleyball team, and was in danger of failing out of college completely.

She slumped around the house, usually sleeping until well after midday, scattering dirty laundry around the place and leaving dishes and soda cans in the living room. Anne kept trying to rally Kayla and get her to do some chores and lose some weight.

The day Kayla went back to school to start her junior year, Anne came to work in tears. She had told Kayla at parting that she was not to come home for Christmas.

"I don't want her in my house anymore," Anne sobbed, *"I hate to say this about my daughter but she's a dirty slob, her grades are bad, she's never had a job, and I don't know what to do about it. I can't have her around anymore. She is just making my life miserable."* Anne is divorced, and she had told Kayla to go stay at her dad's house during Christmas vacation.

Kayla's dad, in his turn, had issued his own ultimatum. His continued financial support was going to be contingent upon Kayla obtaining a 2.5 GPA that semester. If she did not bring her grades up, he intended to withdraw financial support and Kayla could either quit college or fund her own tuition. On one hand, Kayla knew she could not go back to her mother's house. On the other hand, if she went to her father's house with less than a 2.5 GPA, there would be hell to pay — no more money, no more parental support. It was laid out bare for Kayla to reckon with.

I do not want to give the impression that this was easy. Anne was tortured. It is not easy to give ultimatums to your own children. Anne is a good parent, and loves Kayla dearly. She was doing her best, like most of us, to get Kayla off to the right start in life.

At the end of the semester, Anne was thrilled to be able to invite Kayla home for Christmas. Things had changed dramatically from what they were when she left in August. For one thing, Kayla had a job in her college town and was earning pretty good money that paid her rent. Her grades were much better. She had obtained As and Bs that semester instead of Cs and Ds. When she came home, she helped Anne keep the house neat and tidy and did her own laundry. Two years later, Kayla graduated with a very respectable grade point average.

Of course, it does not always work this smoothly. Sometimes there can be a long period of heart wrenching and tough love before a child turns around. But ultimatums, if used sparingly, can jolt our children into the real world and help them reach the next level of maturity. Sometimes they need a chance to break free from the fantasy bubble they have built around themselves. At college, they thought they were free and living large while still depending on mom and dad to pick up the slack and foot the bill. Few of us can afford to give our children this kind of lifestyle and even if we could, we know it is not in our child's best interest.

Naturally, ultimatums should be saved for the last resort after trying logic and reason, and should be used sparingly. One per college degree, if executed adeptly, and timed just right, should be more than enough for your average out-of-control college student. It is called "tough" love for a reason. It is hard to be hard on those we love, especially having raised them from newborn babies, and lovingly watched as they make all their little mistakes and fumbles and still turn into somewhat decent human beings, if a little immature, during the college years. But these final years of teenagers and the early years of adulthood are no less formative than those early years of toddlerhood. Our young adult children are still maturing, learning, and growing — and they need us to be strong.

Accountability

Most of us approach parenting by gently and consistently loosening the reins as children get older and sharply pulling them back if we see them head toward a cliff. But society trains them (and us) to think that when they turn 18, we are going to let go of the reins altogether and let them march on their own steam directly into adulthood. The reality is: it rarely happens this way. At 18, our children still exhibit less than adult maturity, which is only to be expected given the fact that they are still teenagers. It is not a smart tactic to let them go completely. The trick is in allowing them to think they have been let go, and see how they do. If they mess up, rein them back in again.

Once your emerging adult has turned 18, you begin to lose the support of the law and of the educational system. Colleges are not bound to inform you of their grades, and banks are not bound to include you in on their account information. So, there needs to be a good relationship between you and your student if you intend to remain abreast of these finer points in your young adult's new life at college. One thing that seems to work well is financial leverage. *"If you don't tell me what your grades are you can forget allowing me to pay your tuition next semester. You will have to pay your own. After all you are an adult now."* This technique works relatively well for most people. It reminds me of a piece of advice that one student representative on an orientation day for incoming freshmen at Colorado State University was pleased to share with that year's potential recruits. *"Live off your parents as long as you possibly can."* As long as students continue to receive advice like this from their peers and college mentors, parents are still have a decent chance of retaining at least some degree of control.

It is annoying, however, that most schools, while expecting parents to cough up thousands of dollars every semester, make it so hard for us to find out information. The University of Georgia, which conducts 100 percent of their business online, makes no provision for parents to have online accounts. All the information is posted on my son's account, to which only he is supposed to have password access.

All these things contribute to our children feeling they have reached adulthood and must therefore be adults. Unfortunately, college life, by its nature, has fewer restrictions or avenues for accountability than most other adult lifestyles. Contrast a semester of college life, for example, with six months of trying to hold down a full-time job in the real world. It is no wonder that high school graduates who skip college and go straight out to work generally seem more mature after a year or two than many full-time college students.

Senior Year of College

The senior year of college is a strange year for your children. After spending 16 of their 22 years in the education system, they are about to start looking for their first serious job. They will be worrying about having enough credits to graduate, taking final exams, ensuring they take all the necessary steps and meet the necessary college criteria to graduate, talking with career counselors, preparing their resume, and possibly interviewing with potential hiring companies.

The pressure increases every time a family member meets them and innocently asks them "So what are you going to do after graduation?" As nervous as they were about starting college, they feel even more nervous to be released from the safety net of the college system into the big, wide world.

Some students may make the move directly from college to another state to begin work for a new employer in their chosen career field, while others may need to come back home and take the next six months looking for just the right fit. Student loan payments begin after six months. Statistics show that about 75 percent of students are, in fact, employed six months after graduation, but it can take up to a year for some students to find the right kind of job. Do not be surprised if your new graduate has to wait tables or tend bar for a period of time before becoming a full-fledged member of the white collar population.

As parents, we count the days until final graduation so we can finally have what is left of our money to ourselves.

But after four years of having your son or daughter visit only during vacations, it can come as a shock to find they need to not only move back home, but are no better off financially than they were when they left. Far from relieving us from the burden of providing for them financially, we see a dramatic and permanent rise in our utility bills and food bills rather than the occasional surges we have been used to when they were home for vacation.

If you expect your child to move out when college is over, you should be making that clear throughout the college years by referring to it while it is a still distant event sometime in the future. That helps to set the expectation for your child that they will move out as soon as they have found a full-time job. Most children will be planning on this anyway. Some cannot move away quickly enough for their own liking. This is not necessarily a reflection on their relationship with you, but rather an indication that they feel themselves to be mature and competent adults who no longer wish to live dependent on their parents. However, if you have a child who is reluctant to take the steps necessary to move on in their life, you may need to explore the reasons why.

If their reason for wishing to continue living with you is because they do not wish to spend their own money, you may need to have a talk with them. In any case, an adult child living in their parents' house and earning his or her own income should be making financial contributions to the maintenance and expenses of the home. Just how much they should give will depend on your need and their capacity for paying you.

The Boomerang Effect

The boomerang effect is when your adult children come back to live with you after getting their college degree and leaving home. I am not talking about coming back right after they graduate to look for a job. That part is natural and necessary, even if we forget to think about it for the four years they are at school. The boomerang effect refers to grown children that revert back to living with their parents after a period of true independence. Sometimes they bring a spouse or their children with them and you have to start all over again helping them get on their feet and regain their independence. There can be several reasons. Lack of funds due to a low paying job or a spell of unemployment is one reason. Another may be the break-up of a relationship, possibly a divorce, and they have nowhere else to go while they try and pull their life back together.

Some parents welcome the opportunity to have their adult children rejoin the household. They like the life in the house; perhaps they welcome the chance to interact once more with their children or spend time with their grandchildren. But this model does not encourage young adults to stand on their own and learn how to properly provide for their own children.

Other parents do not want their children to move back in but feel in a tight corner when things go wrong for their children. It is hard to tell your children that you do not want them back. It is hard to set the expectation that they must cope for themselves unless there is a case of true hardship, like their house burning down, for example. Even then, a responsible adult should have adequate insurance coverage!

The expectations we set for our children begin early on. It is probably too late to casually mention it to them as they pile the last of their belongings into the U-Haul six months following graduation. *"Well enjoy your new home kiddo and I hope you never move back here again."* It is better to set the stage throughout their life by casually mentioning now and again that one day after they graduate college you expect to be able to pay them visits in their home. Chances are, over the course of their life, they will develop their own sense that it is not the right thing to do, and they will not want to move back into your house after striking out on their own. With a good education and good job prospects, they should be able to stand on their own two feet and should not need to revert back to depending on their parents.

I am not saying that I would not welcome my children back into my home, but I think they are clear on the fact that I do not expect them to return, and I do not think they will want to. But life happens, and if one of them had a real need, I would make them welcome, while at the same time letting them know that I would expect it to be a temporary arrangement.

Raising Children Is Like Whipping Cream

Have you ever whipped fresh cream? Fresh cream is runny and thin. If you put if on pumpkin pie, it runs right off, just like milk. But if you whip it up long enough, it turns into a rich, fluffy, creamy mound that is several times bigger in volume than what you started with and sticks deliciously to the pie. When you begin to whip it with an electric mixer, it starts to increase in volume rather slowly. In fact, it takes a long time. About five long minutes after you started thinking about giving up because it is too much trouble, it starts to thicken and retain the impression of the beater. You beat and beat, and still it is not quite whipped yet. If you stop too soon, and set it aside, it will start to decompose and turn back to liquid. If you have the patience to wait until it is truly whipped, it will retain its rich, fluffy texture for a week in the refrigerator. You can tell when it is done because the smooth texture of the cream changes. This is called "breaking." When the cream breaks, add a little sugar and you are done. But reaching that breaking point can seem to take all the patience that you have.

Teenagers, between 18 and 20 (or even up to age 22 and beyond), are like cream in that final stage, right before it breaks. You want to stop raising them, and they want you to stop raising them. But if you stop now, all your work will decompose and turn to water. You need to find the patience and the strength deep inside to keep raising them until they turn to cream. Then they will keep their shape forever and you can let them go with confidence.

CHAPTER 18

Revitalizing Your Life

Whether you have sent your first child or your last off to college, you are probably realizing that you have been a parent most of your adult life. The point here is that you have little recollection of your adult hobbies or interests before you were a parent. Even if you remember what you used to like doing, chances are you have forgotten how to do it or are out of practice.

Every decision you have made for the last 18 or more years, you have taken into consideration how it will impact the children. When people asked you what your hobbies are you said things like *"Helping with the swim team,"* or *"Spending time with the family."*

Even though our children have not died, they have simply grown up, something we have looked forward to all our lives, we need to pass through a sort of mourning period for the loss of their childhood.

I remember when my third and last child potty-trained. I had spent eight years in a row changing diapers. I had it down to a fine art. I could do it inconspicuously practically anywhere: on a plane, in a crowded shopping mall, or at the home of a friend. I was a diaper-changing expert. After Christopher started using the toilet on a regular basis, I sobbed inconsolably. Nobody could figure out what was wrong with me. Everyone thought I should be happy that I would no longer have to change diapers. But I felt an overwhelming sense of loss because I thought my children no longer needed me.

I Had Simply Done It for too Long

Once I got used to the change and realized my children still needed me, I was finally able to experience the heady freedom that came with being rid of the diaper bag.

Our children leaving for college is just another of those life changing, pivotal moments. But they are still our children, we are still their parents, and they will always need us — just for different reasons now that they are grown.

Joy explains her mixed feelings when Heather left for college in the following way:

> "I was looking forward to having my daughter out on her own, but at the same time, dreading having my daughter out on her own. Knowing she was inexperienced with the world, I knew she would have questions and problems that I would have to deal with from afar. I was looking forward to being on my own, too, but knowing all along that I would really miss her."

It is natural to miss our children when they leave, but we must remember that we were never raising them to spend the rest of their lives living under our roof, and we knew all along that the day was coming when they would strike out on their own.

It is only college. It is not as if we will never see them again. Indeed, at the end of the summer you will be just as pleased to see them go back to college (as you were to see them go back to school so that you could get them out from under your feet) and get back to that nice, calm peace you have become used to.

Having spent the better part of your adult life raising them, sometimes it comes as quite a shock to realize that it is all over and now it is your turn. This is the time you waited for; you are able to do things without worrying whether it is going to affect the children. It is here at last.

Have Patience

It takes time to find new interests, develop new friends, and build a new life. The child-raising years can be full of family events, sporting events, school meetings, and so on. We are constantly busy and we often pass through several years in a row with no time to ourselves. So much so that we do not even notice that we have made few new friends in recent years and have fallen out of touch with old ones. Most of our interaction has been with our immediate family or perhaps the parents of our children's friends. So when our children leave home and all the activity that was centered around child-raising suddenly grinds to a halt, we can become frustrated that it is taking so long to build a new life.

The sooner you get started on the process by getting out and about to find new activities and new people in your life, the sooner things will happen and both you and your student will benefit. But it does not happen overnight. After a few years of rebuilding you will look back and see you have come a long way, but in the meantime there may be some months of inactivity, of nowhere new to go, and no one new to meet with.

Remember that you need to kindle friendships, both new and old, but especially new ones. You will sometimes have to invite other people to several things before they begin to invite you back. You will have to make an effort to be the first one to get in touch. If they do not call back or e-mail you back right away, you may need to get in touch with them again. There may be contacts who you would like to continue meeting with but do not reciprocate or respond, and you have drop those and start over with someone else. Not everyone is in the same situation as you. When you meet new people, sometimes those people will already have full lives and may not notice your efforts to make friends.

A year may pass and you may realize that you have only met with your new friend once or twice all year. In fact, it may take five years before a close friendship starts to emerge.

As an adult, breaking into new friendships can be hard

work. Perhaps you are comfortable with your spouse and close relatives and you have forgotten how long it takes to trust new friends and become close. We remember how easy it seemed as children. When a new child moved in across the street you just hung out in the street and pretty soon you ran into them, and the easy way we just said "Hi, I'm Jim, what's your name?" and the friendship was off and running. It is not as easy as an adult.

As adults, we cocoon ourselves inside family life, or we find that some of our friends, such as those we know from work, gradually developed over a period of years working alongside someone and having regular daily contact with them.

Enjoy the Quiet Times

If you happen to find yourself in a waiting period where it is taking time to break new ground and form new friendships, it is a good time to enjoy the solitude, or the quiet times. What seems like deathly silence when your child first leaves for college will soon seem like heavenly peace when they go back to start their sophomore year after being home for the summer.

This is a good time to do something like re-explore your taste in music. When was the last time you discovered a new band or a new kind of music you enjoy listening to? When was the last time you went to a concert? Or it may be a good time to visit the local library and check out a few good books to listen to, or some audio tapes to listen to in the car, now that you no longer have to tune it to your child's favorite music station or plug his iPod into your car stereo.

Start to Dream Again

Now is the time to create some momentum for your own dreams. Remember all those times you have stood at the sink washing dishes or waited patiently in the car by the gym for them to get out soccer practice? Did you sit and dream about all the things you would do with your life when this time was over?

The first step to rekindling the momentum is to reawaken our dreams. We have spent so much of our time dreaming on behalf of our children, have we not? We have dreamt about what college they will go to, how they will manage away from home, and what kind of people they will become. It is time to turn the spotlight back to ourselves. Think of all the things you meant to do in your life. Have you done them? Think of all the things you wanted and did not buy because you had to find money for a baseball tour, an orchestra camp, or a hockey tournament. Write yourself a list of all the things you would like to do, a list of things to help you be the person you would like to become, or a list of the places you would like to go.

We all have dreams. The hardest part is moving them into reality. Perhaps you have always wanted to start your own business but were afraid of taking the risk because you needed to keep a roof over your children's heads. Or perhaps you have always wanted to volunteer for a worthy cause, but you could never find the time in between being the taxi-driver, the homework coach, the cheerleading section, and director of the college application process.

I remember my father tried several times to get his own business off the ground while we were at home. When I was quite small, I remember going with him to look at premises that held the potential to become a TV shop. He turned down promotions to avoid moving across the country and settled for a lower salary to offer us a stable environment and avoid the disruption of changing high schools. Of course, at the time I did not see it that way. But after all his children had left home, his home business took off. My dad died working, doing what he loved, and running his own business. It was only much later on, when I looked back as an adult, that I realized what a sacrifice he had made for us children while we were small. He denied himself his own dreams to give us our chance. But he followed his dream in the end.

Most of us have stories of our own of things we did not do, opportunities we knowingly passed on, and plans we set aside while we focused on raising our children and getting them off to a good start. These are the hallmarks of responsible parenting. But we are so used to sacrificing and focusing on them that sometimes it is hard to gain back the momentum. We tell ourselves we are too old now or we do not need the money any more. Well, we are not too old, and we do need the money. All we need to make it work is to create a little momentum for our dreams, and there is plenty of time left to create a completely new life for ourselves.

Developing Hobbies and Interests

There is no time like the present. The easiest way to get back into our own lives is to do something positive. Take a single step in the direction you want to go. Do not give yourself reasons for not doing something. Do not tell yourself, "I'll look into it after Christmas." Why wait? Start right now.

Do not put it off. There must be something you have always wanted to do. If you do not work, get a part-time job doing something that looks like fun, then go, and enjoy doing it. If you work full-time, become a volunteer. There are so many rewarding ways to give your time back to your community; you are bound to find something you enjoy. When you volunteer for something it is like playing when you were a child. It is pure fun. There is no pressure. Get involved with something and see where it takes you. If you find it becomes a chore or you are not enjoying it, find something else. Because when you find something that you love, it is never a chore and you look forward to it.

If you do not want to go out and volunteer for something, perhaps you have always wanted to collect something, learn to play an instrument, or learn a new language. Do some research. Ask your older friends what they are involved with and what their interests are.

Here are some ideas to get your mind working on all the possibilities for re-energizing your life.

- **Volunteer at an elementary school.** Think of

all the good you can do now that you are older and wiser and have first-hand experience of how early learning sets us up for our future.

- **Volunteer at your church.** There are always opportunities to get involved with your local church, whether it is singing in the choir, sitting on the financial advisory board, or visiting people of the parish who have lost a loved one or are housebound.

- **Get a part-time job.** Whether you work full-time or part-time or stay at home because you do not have to work, there are some fun and rewarding experiences to be had working part-time. One woman I know who teaches elementary school works part-time at a baseball stadium selling peanuts. She loves the experience — to get out and meet some adults and "throw peanuts at them." Another great idea is to work part-time at a department store. For a few hours a week, you can get a great sales discount and make some new friends into the bargain.

- **Volunteer as a teacher.** The whole world loves teachers. Now that we are older, have lived in the world, and have raised our children, we have so much experience that we should be sharing with the next generation, as well as with our peers. Teaching children and adults can be a rewarding experience and can lead to deep satisfaction and fulfillment. If you are already a teacher, you know this. If you have never taught, there are many opportunities for volunteers.

- **Become a Big Sister or a Big Brother.** You can find out more about this wonderful mentoring organization at **http://www.bbbs.org.**

- **If you work full-time, and you do not want to commit to volunteering or a second job,** you could simply choose a young person at work to mentor. You will feel a lot of satisfaction mentoring someone who is roughly the same age as your absent student. It will keep you in touch with how the younger generation is thinking and behaving, and it can help you feel more in touch with your own student.

- **Finally, if you cannot find a link to something that interests you,** consider setting up your own organization, club, or support group. Contact your friends, get on the Internet, and figure out the first steps. Your local library may offer free meeting rooms for non-profit organizations and will help you with flyer distribution.

Motivation

The difference between a good idea and a successful project is simply doing it.

As Walt Disney put it:

*"The way to get started is to quit talking
and begin doing."*

One way to motivate yourself is to write down all the benefits of your idea once it is implemented. Consider all the ways in which your life will be richer and more meaningful. Then write down all the negatives of not taking action. Include things like how bored you will be, how lonely you will be, and how you will have nothing new to talk about with your friends, your spouse, and your students when they come back home. You do not have to think about how you will implement your idea when you go through this exercise. Just imagine it is already somehow magically implemented and try to envision how much you will be enjoying it.

When you have found your motivation, use that to propel yourself into action.

Start by creating some goals for yourself. Break the ultimate objective down into some easy steps. For instance, if you think you might like to take a part-time job, the first step will be finding just the right job. Maybe you would like to do some part-time writing, work in a department store, or give a yoga class at the YMCA.

Next, you will need to research what you need to do to get there. If you intend to give exercise classes, you will need to be certified. If you want to work in a department store, you can usually submit an online application from your home computer. If you want to write part-time, you will need to do some research to find out who is looking for the topics you are interested in writing about.

Develop all your goals on paper and continue to break down into steps the things you need to do to reach your objectives. The research alone can sometimes be fun and lead you to places you had not even considered. Do not forget to implement the steps after you define them. That is the whole point of the exercise — and that is how you turn a dream into reality.

Above all, remember that it is all for fun, for your own leisure, and for enjoyment, so if it becomes too much of a chore or is not a pleasure, then you have not found quite the right thing. Keep looking and researching until just the right thing comes along.

I attempted many different volunteer jobs until I found the one that was right for me. Some I did for weeks, and some I only did once or twice. When I found what I like I have kept doing it, and now it is one of my greatest sources of strength and fulfillment. Among the things I tried: volunteering as a facilitator for a divorce working group, mentoring disadvantaged youth, volunteering on the financial committee of a local church, and working part-time in the retail industry. Now I teach English as a second language to adult immigrants, and I find this work fascinating and interesting. I love trying to make sense of our English language as I explain it to others, and I enjoy learning about the diversity of other cultures and learning about the experiences of other people, what drove them to seek a better life in a new country, what they have been through in their lives to get here and to provide a better life for their loved ones. You, too, will find something fulfilling and rewarding.

Returning to Work after Staying Home

For some mothers, and even for some fathers too, our life's work has been staying home to raise our children. We elected not to go outside of the home to work, choosing instead to dedicate ourselves to raising our children. Some of us may have also home-schooled our children.

If this is the case, you may feel especially empty and lonely once your children go off to college. It can be as though the meaning for your existence is over. If you are a single mother, it can also mark the end of child support and going back to work may be a necessity to increase your income. Do not worry; your life is not over. It is just beginning.

Someone who is good at planning their life and setting goals for themselves may have already been preparing for a return to work by taking some classes, going back to school to get a degree, or networking with friends to figure out what the job market is like. If you have not been laying plans for yourself and you would like (or need) to go back to work after a long absence, there are steps you can take to help yourself get back in the work force.

The first thing to do is to sit down and think about any reasons that may be holding you back or creating stumbling blocks in your path. Here are some of the most common reasons we vacillate:

- I am too old; no one will hire me.

- I have no experience — I cannot do anything.

- I do not know what I want to do.

- I do not think I will enjoy working.

- I am too out of touch with my profession.

Let us break down these obstacles one by one.

I am too old; no one will hire me.

It is probably true that a generation ago it was harder for older members of the workforce to get certain types of jobs. That has changed. There is an explosion of jobs available over the Internet, for example. There is worldwide movement toward globalization, and many companies large and small are creating a presence in multiple different countries and states. This means employers will hire people local to certain areas who report to a boss located on the other side of the country. You may not even meet your boss face-to-face when you are hired. A person can do many things without ever meeting their employer. If you structure your resume properly and interview by telephone, your employer will not necessarily form an idea of how old you are. Even if they do, it is less likely to stand in your way.

One friend I know went back to college when her youngest son started high school. She had stayed home with him all his life. While her son was in high school, she studied for her master's degree. After he went to college, she graduated and found herself a high-paying job. She was 58 when she returned to work after raising her children. She is now happily employed and enjoying a great income! What an inspiration to the rest of us!

I have no experience — I cannot do anything.

If you have stayed home to raise your children, you have developed many skills. Let me name a few:

- **Budgeting:** You have had to manage on a budget (possibly a tight one) and ensure the family was well provided for in terms of food, school supplies, clothes, home maintenance, entertainment, car maintenance, and so on. This means you have developed skills for prioritizing, planning, and forecasting (how to afford Christmas and get the roof fixed in the same year).

- **Team Building and Personnel Skills:** You have been the focal point of the family and kept the family bond strong through good and hard times. You have learned how to leverage your children's skills (getting them to fix the computer for you) and motivate them to be productive (cleaning their room).

- **Management:** You are a multi-tasker extraordinaire, and you have developed exceptional organizational skills. You have effectively found ways to ensure family attendance at your son's band performance, your daughter's dance recital, and pick your best friend's son up from soccer practice all on the same night. You managed to nourish and nurture multiple family members when all were flying in different directions to fulfill their obligations and meet their deadlines, and you were able to keep up the laundry and make sure the right child was wearing the right uniform for the right function on the right day 99 percent of the time.

- **Conflict Resolution:** Remember that time when your husband and your daughter did not talk for three days and you helped them reconcile? Or when your son and your daughter got into one of their worst fights ever and accidentally broke your antique vase and you had to control your own anger long enough to sort out who started it, what the issue was, and how to resolve it? If you think back, you will remember numerous incidents where you had to think fast and respond quickly. You will remember times when you were the most hated one for doling out some punishment that was deemed unfair, or where you reprimanded yourself for not punishing severely enough. If you think adults in the workplace behave differently than siblings fighting over who got the biggest slice of cake, you are sadly mistaken. Indeed, I think raising children has put me in a better position for management than all the college-level management classes I have taken.

These are some of the skills you may have developed while raising your family. I am sure you will be able to think of more if you stop and consider all the things you have had to learn to do and deal with over the years.

I do not know what I want to do.

It is difficult to decide what to do after you have had an absence from the workplace. If you worked before you stayed home, you may consider returning to your previous field, even if you start out in a role of less seniority than what you may have achieved previously. Once you get back into it you may find that it has not changed all that much, or that you come back to your field with a fresh mind, ready for learning, and you may be able to progress reasonably quickly back to where you were before.

But it is also reasonable to look for something different altogether. Many people who remain in the work force all their lives change careers three or more times these days. We all evolve and need to re-evaluate where we are in our lives periodically. Think about the things you like to do and what you are good at, and then try to discover what types of jobs offer you the opportunity to incorporate all of it.

One exercise that can help is to go to a job search Web site such as **http://www.monster.com.** Put some keywords into the search engine related to the type of work you would like and see what you come up with. Most posted jobs come with job descriptions. Read some job descriptions for jobs you think you might qualify for and see if they sound interesting to you.

This is also a good way to find out what qualifications you need for the jobs you are thinking about, and to determine whether you need to go back to school.

Another thing to try is to go to a freelance Web site such as **http://www.elance.com** or **http://www.guru.com** and look into the types of jobs that you could do from home using your computer. Chances are, if you have been out the workforce for a while, you will find a completely new world of employment opportunities out there that you did not even realize existed.

I do not think I will enjoy working.

You want to work — you want the distraction, and you want the money, but you have made a comfortable life for yourself at home and you think it may be too wrenching to hold down a tight work schedule five days a week. Even though there is not too much to do at home any more now that the children have gone, you are not quite ready to take a total plunge back into the rat race.

I know several people who do paid work for charity organizations. This work can be fulfilling and give you a tremendous sense of doing something worthwhile and interesting. Many jobs, whether for-profit or not-for-profit, offer alternative work schedules and part-time opportunities. Part-time can be anything from a few hours a week to 30 or 35 hours. If you chose a 30-hour-a-week schedule you would qualify for full medical benefits in many organizations and could choose to work three days for 10 hours a day, or six hours a day five days a week, or some other schedule. You may even be allowed to vary it from week to week.

If you do not want to work and you do not need to, then of course you should not. However, if you are making an excuse because you are nervous or worried about returning to work, then you need to realize that there are many way to go back to work and many more options and possibilities than there were 20 years ago. The workplace has changed.

I am too out of touch with my profession.

Depending on your level of commitment and motivation, it is certainly possible, even after a protracted absence, to get back into your previous line of work and to expect a steady increase in compensation. You will get what you settle for, so do not settle for less than you know you should. You will have to be proactive to get your income back up. No one is going to give you a huge pay raise unless you set goals and move confidently toward them. That may include asking for raises rather than sitting back and waiting for them, or changing jobs to get a jump in your salary.

We tend to define ourselves by the company we keep. If you have stayed home for a period you probably identify yourself as a stay-at-home parent, and your friends may be in the same position as yourself. There is no need to abandon your friends, but you should consider broadening your circle to include professional men and women in the line of work you would like to go after. This is not just for networking, although that is an interesting side effect of finding new friends. The primary reason is you want their attitudes and insights to rub off on you. No matter what line of work you are in, there is an insider language, culture, and unwritten code of conduct. If you want to make a serious attempt to break into that circle, it is important to study the culture, absorb the language, and learn the rules.

You can go to your local library or get on the Internet and search for organizations in your area that you may be able to apply to for membership. As an example, the chamber of commerce has local lunches that will expose you to networking possibilities with people from a diverse range of professions. Bring your spouse, your mother, or a friend, but do not be afraid to go alone. Plenty of professionals attend these things alone — that is sort of the point. If you go with someone, you will be less inclined to speak to other people and other people will be less inclined to approach you.

Ask people about themselves and what they do, and do not be afraid or shy to tell them about yourself and let them know you are trying to re-enter the work force. Before you go, you should prepare your "elevator" speech — a short summary of your skills and accomplishments to use when you introduce yourself to people. You want to keep it short enough to memorize, but descriptive enough to give people a good idea of what you want to do. That way they can help you network with others who may be seeking someone with your skills.

You can also research other organizations in your area specific to your profession. For example, if you are a woman in the engineering field, you could search for a chapter of the Society of Women Engineers or Women in Defense, which would offer lunch and other social opportunities for getting to know women in the engineering and defense fields. If you were previously in real estate, there may be a local Association of Realtors, and so on. You may also consider getting involved in organizations like the Rotary Foundation and Toastmasters International, which are both non-profit organizations that offer tremendous opportunities for giving back while you brush up on your networking skills, your public speaking skills, and make some new friends.

CHAPTER 19

Re-feathering the Nest

The best part of sending your children off to college is getting your house back. At first, you wander around the quiet, empty house, peek in their lonely rooms, and hear the echo of happy memories lingering in the hallway. For the last 18 years or more, your entire life has been dedicated to making sacrifices, putting them first, and putting your own life on hold. Perhaps you redecorated their bedrooms several times as they grew up, but never redecorated your own? Or perhaps you have been meaning to replace an old couch in the family room, but you were waiting until the children grew out of the putting-their-feet-up-on-it stage?

Roll up Your Sleeves and Get on with It

A friend of mine was depressed when her last child went off to college. A single mom, she felt completely alone, rattling around the house all by herself. I asked her what she had always wanted to do to the house. She confessed that even though she desperately missed her daughters, their rooms were an absolute mess. She resented the fact that both her daughters had gone off and left her to go to college, and yet they had left her with this monumental mess in two rooms of her house and she did not know how to begin to deal with it. She did not like to tidy up their things for fear of upsetting her daughters on their return, and she was afraid to throw anything away in case it had some kind of meaning or value.

Together we brainstormed a solution. She put a big box in each room and started to clean out the rooms. She organized what she could, dusted and cleaned every surface, vacuumed the carpet and under the bed, and everything she was not sure what to do with she put in the box. After a couple of days of cleaning, she had both rooms neat and orderly and a pleasure to look in upon. Neatly tucked in each bedroom closet was a big box of miscellaneous items. When her daughters came home, their first thought was that she had thrown out their stuff. But when she showed them the boxes, they thanked her for tidying up and admitted their rooms looked really nice.

It is all right to reclaim your space. You student is off to college and having a grand old time. There is no need to sit at home and mope in your own house. Reclaim your space. You do not have to kick your offspring out of the home. Just re-establish your right to it. They are old enough to realize they cannot live there forever.

Spruce the Place up a Bit

Perhaps while your children were growing up and tearing around the house on their tricycles and rollerblades, playing trampoline on their bed, or rough housing on the sofa, you were reluctant to replace things as they became worn or broken. After all, what is the point of re-upholstering a favorite chair or re-carpeting the family room when you know all it takes is a single spilled glass of purple Kool-Aid or a small (accidental, of course) rip with a penknife or a pair of scissors to give it that lived-in look?

This is no time to be sentimental and hang on to your old stuff because it is full of happy memories. Let the memories live in your heart and get yourself a new leather sofa to sit on or a new high-definition TV to watch. Clean out the garage or your closet, and take some stuff to a charity store. Then go out and buy something new to replace it.

Even a small ornament or knick-knack will give you a lift and will be something new to look at around the house so that you do not sit around feeling sorry for yourself.

When Should You Convert Their Bedroom into a Den?

If your children have not left home yet, you do not need to make drastic changes around the house. It is good to make small, gradual changes — redo the kitchen or redecorate the living room. But you probably do not want to convert their bedroom into a den until they have truly moved out of the house. Going away to college is not moving out. College students sometimes feel like they are in limbo. They are not living at home any more, but a dorm room in a residence hall does not feel like home either. It is not their own. They get locked out of it at Christmas and kicked out completely every May. They need their home base and some continuity in their life at this fragile and vulnerable time.

It is a balance between sprucing things up by refreshing a few pieces of furniture to give yourself a nice, comfortable environment and keeping things the way they were so your children feel like they are coming home and not visiting a strange house.

When to kick your children out of the nest is one of those topics that people tend to feel strongly about. I am not one of those parents who would kick my children out of the house the minute they turn 18 or 21. However, once they graduate college and have had a year or two to settle down and start making some money, I will encourage them to leave. I want my children to feel welcome in their own home whenever they come back from college and so I will not redecorate their room, turn it into a sewing room, or re-allocate it as a guest bedroom until they take it upon themselves to set up house elsewhere. However, everyone feels differently on this topic.

After your children move on, if you have been helping them with college expenses, you should find yourself with more money to spare and more space. It is a good time to think about major renovations — a new kitchen, a remodeled bathroom, or converting the children bedrooms into something else.

A New Set of Wheels

By the time most of us get our children through high school and college we have not only spent a great deal of money, we have also gone through several vehicles. Some get wrecked along the way, others sputter to a grinding halt along the highway, and some are pressed into service in distant college towns, carefully selected for their ability to handle long cross-country trips under the weight of one student's entire collection of dorm room furnishings and personal belongings.

I remember a co-worker proudly showing off his new red sports car, a BMW. This elderly gentleman could not have been more proud of his new vehicle. He recounted with graphic detail how many used cars he went through while his two sons were in college. Some were burned through by his boys in a flurry of incidents that would make any parent's hair stand on end. Some he bought on the used market to drive himself, and they simply sputtered to a halt because they were old.

"Now that I no longer have college expenses to pay for," he beamed, "I have earned this reward."

I personally have been reluctant to buy a new car while my boys are in college, not just because of the expense a new car brings, but because somewhere in the back of my mind I suspect that sooner or later I will have to turn it over to one of my sons to bail them out of a tight spot. Even if I later get it back, I know it will come home battered and bruised.

If you are finally at the end of your college expenses, there is nothing like the smell of a new car to reward yourself for the great job you have done as a parent and raising your fine young adults.

Your Child's Appreciation

There is a side effect that results from you taking care of your own needs, fixing up your home, and buying yourself a new car. Your children, who begin to see you as adults rather than parents only when they achieve adulthood themselves, begin to deepen their appreciation of your sacrifice. When they see parents who are in or near retirement start to enjoy luxuries they could never previously afford, children begin to understand what it has taken for you to support them. They gain a much better appreciation for home and what it means to be family because of being away from it.

I remember noticing small things around my parent's house that began to clue me in on my parents' new financial freedom. Foods they never used to buy, because they were too expensive, started to appear in their fridge. My father had always wanted to run his own business but was always afraid to take the risk while he had children to support. After his children left home, he took the chance and developed a thriving accounting practice out of his home. I had vague recollections of his conversations with my mother when he discussed the risks and potential rewards, and always decided to err on the safe side so he would be able to put us through school. These memories would come flooding back to me as I realized, in my twenties and later, exactly how much of his own life he had put on hold for me. Now I see myself doing the same thing for my own children as he did for me.

It All Works Out

When Heather graduated from college, Joy was surprised at how much her daughter had grown up when she looked back through her memories of the four college years.

> *"I am still so surprised at how much my daughter grew up and took responsibility for herself! I enjoy her more now than I ever did when she was a teenager in high school."*

Janet reported that when her son, Ryan, went off to college she was worried about him. He left a small town in Colorado to attend college in the heart of a big East Coast city. But he instantly grew up and thirsted for knowledge both in his academic studies and in his personal life.

> *"He wanted to become as independent as possible by learning to do things on his own. For example, after his car broke down a couple of times, he bought a manual to learn how to repair his car."*

Although she was worried when he first went off to college, in the end and looking back, Janet thinks that it went much better than she imagined. With two sons who have now graduated from college, she thinks her grown sons are much closer to her than they were when they lived at home:

> *"Going off to college is one of the best*

ways for teenagers to mature, become independent, and learn what they need to know to get by in the world. Without parents being there to fix everything, they learn to figure things out on their own. It is very rewarding to see them grow into responsible adults. "

The Reward

There finally comes a time in every parent's life when children graduate college, go off and find useful employment, and move out of the parental home (hopefully for good). At this point, if you have not already done so, reclaim your living space entirely and use it any way you wish. Perhaps you want to use one bedroom as a guest room; another can be converted into a sewing room, a reading room, or a playroom for the grandchildren.

Your money is finally your own and you can finally buy that BMW or Lexus that you have been dreaming of, take a cruise, or put in wall-to-wall carpeting in the basement or wood paneling in the family room.

You can sit back on your laurels and look forward to retirement, knowing you have done your part to raise responsible adults who will go forth and prosper in the world and who, in their turn, will create the next wave of progress and the next generation of the human race.

While small and immediate rewards gradually make themselves apparent throughout the college years and as we follow those final maturing steps our children take toward fully-fledged adulthood, many parents report the best rewards lie even further in the future. Some of us do not fully mature until we hit our thirties, and for some, it takes having children of our own, at whatever age that turns out to be. Parents often report that their children become closer to them after they leave home.

The rewards come at different times in isolated moments. You may be watching your daughter wrestling to tie her wriggling toddler's shoe — and for a brief moment in her frustrated expression, you see yourself when your daughter was a toddler. It may be in a special Christmas gift that your grown son gives you, an expensive watch perhaps, and while looking down into the shiny watch face you catch a reflection of your own tired features, and remember all you have gone through to bring your child to the point of lavishing expensive luxuries on his parent.

If
By Rudyard Kipling

If you can keep your head when all about you
Are losing theirs and blaming it on you,
If you can trust yourself when all men doubt you,
But make allowance for their doubting too;

If you can wait and not be tired by waiting,
Or being lied about, don't deal in lies,
Or being hated don't give way to hating,
And yet don't look too good, nor talk too wise:

If you can dream — and not make dreams your master;
If you can think — and not make thoughts your aim;
If you can meet with Triumph and Disaster
And treat those two imposters just the same.

If
By Rudyard Kipling

If you can make one heap of all your winnings
And risk it on one turn of pitch and toss,
And lose, and start again at your beginnings
And never breathe a word about your loss.

If you can talk with crowds and keep your virtue
Or walk with Kings — nor lose the common touch,
If neither foes nor loving friends can hurt you,
If all men count with you, but none too much;

If you can fill the unforgiving minute
With sixty seconds' worth of distance run,
Yours is the Earth and everything that's in it,
And — which is more — you'll be a Man, my son!

From *Rewards and Fairies* by Rudyard Kipling, 1910

Bibliography

Andrea Van Steenhouse, Ph. D. *Empty Nest Full Heart: The Journey from Home to College*, Simpler Life Press, 1998.

Carol Barkin. *When Your Kid Goes To College: A Parents Survival Guide*, Avon Books, 1999.

Robin Raskin. "A Parents' Guide to College Life," The Princeton Review Inc, 2006.

Laura S. Kastner, Ph.D. and Jennifer Wyatt, Ph.D. *The Launching Years*, Clarkson Potter/Publishers, New York, New York, 2002.

Marjorie Savage. *You're On Your Own (But I'm Here if You Need Me): Mentoring Your Child Through the College Years*, A Fireside book, 2003.

Margo E. Bane Woodacre, MSW & Steffany Bane. *I'll Miss You Too (An Off-to-College Guide for Parents and Students)*, Sourcebooks, Inc. 2006.

Karen Levin Coburn and Madge Lawrence Treeger. *Letting Go — A Parent's Guide to Understanding the College Years*, Fourth Edition, 2003.

Michael J. Leonard, Division of Undergraduate Studies, Penn State University, Created January 1, 1996; Revised May 5, 2006, **http://www.psu.edu/dus/md/mdintro. htm.**

Rudyard Kipling. "If," *Rewards and Fairies*, 1910

Rudyard KiplingIna Sivits Lurning. "What Should Parents Expect From Their Student The First Few Weeks Of Semester?" Mental Health, University Housing, **http:// housing.unl.edu/parents/expectations.shtml.**

Georgia Tech University. *The Georgia Tech Parents Handbook*, Georgia Tech Parents Program, **http:// gtamlumni.org/parents.**

Colorado State University, *Colorado State University Parent's Handbook,* **http://www.day.colostate.edu/ parents.asp.**

Author Biography

Mary Spohn graduated from the University of Bath in Great Britain. She came to the United States from Great Britain in 1981 and attended San Jose State University in California where she studied Computer Science. She currently works as a Computer Systems Architect in Colorado Springs, Colorado. The college application process is very different in England than in the United States and so when her three children were in the process of applying to colleges, Mary made a committed effort to research and understand all the nuances of the college application process. As a result, she has been able to help other parents who are currently undertaking the process with their children.

Index